D0810587

The Three Voyages of
Captain Cook

CAPTAIN JAMES COOK, F.R.S.

ENGRAVED BY J. BASIRE IN 1777

From a painting by William Hodges

The Three Voyages of Captain Cook

Frank Paluka

BETA PHI MU

1974

Beta Phi Mu Chapbook Number Ten
Published by Beta Phi Mu, Pittsburgh, Pennsylvania
ISBN 0-910230-10-2

Library of Congress Cataloging Information follows:

Paluka, Frank.
  The three voyages of Captain Cook.

  (Beta Phi Mu chapbook no. 10)
  Includes bibliographical references.
  1. Cook, James, 1728-1779. 2. Pacific Ocean.
I. Title. II. Series.
G246.C7P34   910.09'164'0924 ⌐B⌐   73-88544
ISBN 0-910230-10-2

Library of Congress Catalog Card Number: 73-88544

For
Chris, Steve, Dana
and Derek

CONTENTS

FOREWORD

BETA PHI MU, the national library science honorary fraternity, began publishing its chapbooks twenty years ago and as
The Three Voyages of Captain Cook is No. 10 in the series,
this averages out to one every two years. Not that there has
been any biennial scheduling; the fraternity publishes only
when members of the selection committee find a manuscript
which they believe suits their objective of combining the
literature of books and libraries with the art of book design.

With Frank Paluka as author, the number of librarians who
have written chapbooks for the series reaches five, or exactly
half the total, which seems to be a sensible proportion. For the
past ten years, Mr. Paluka has been head of the Special Collections Department in the University of Iowa Libraries. Before
that he was a wandering scholar, having departed his native
Iowa at the age of 17 as an army enlistee. After serving with
the Twentieth Air Force in the Marianas Islands, he became a
student and teacher, sometimes both concurrently, at Creigh-
ton University, University of Connecticut, Florida State University, and the University of Illinois. He published *Iowa
Authors* in 1967, and has been editor of *Books at Iowa* since
1966.

The designer for this chapbook is Michael Stancik, Jr., who
has won awards from American Institute of Graphic Arts,

Society of Typographic Arts, and the Chicago Book Clinic. Among publishers who have used his work are Yale University Press, Chicago Historical Society, Notre Dame Press, and the Coverdale Press. For typographic experimentation, Mr. Stancik operates his own press (Trinity Press) in Chicago, and he collects first editions of well-designed books.

PREFACE

OF HIS THREE major voyages of exploration James Cook himself wrote narrative accounts which have survived. In addition, on all of these voyages a number of Cook's companions kept journals of their own which add details not to be found in the "official" publications. Particularly notable in this regard are the journals of Joseph Banks and of Sydney Parkinson on the first voyage; of Anders Sparrman and the two Forsters on the second voyage; and of David Samwell on the third voyage.

It has seemed a useful undertaking to draw upon the best of these first-hand accounts in order to piece together a single brief narrative which should attempt to suggest the amplitude and excitement of these remarkable eighteenth-century explorations. Some coherence, it was thought, might likewise be found among the many specialized Cook studies of modern times by relating them to the context provided by a narrative overview. It is thus the aim of the present little book not only to trace Cook's routes geographically but, through a survey of the literature, to invite attention to the best of the many-faceted works which study the historical, scientific, personal, and artistic consequences of the three voyages of Captain Cook.

With few exceptions my footnote citations may be accepted as recommended readings; they attempt to single out works which are worth pursuing. The serious student will also want to consult at least two other bibliographies. Sir Maurice Holmes' *Captain James Cook, R.N., F.R.S., A Bibliographical Excursion* (London, 1952; reprinted New York, 1968) is for the most part a chronologically arranged listing of primary works of the eighteenth century; it nonetheless includes highly selective notices of nineteenth- and twentieth-century works, and its comments are models of succinct annotation. *The Bibliography of Captain James Cook, R.N., F.R.S., Circumnavigator*, published by the Mitchell Library of New South Wales, should be used in its vastly expanded second edition of 1970. It is notable for its comprehensiveness and its full index.

Occasional brief quotations in the ensuing pages for which I give no specific footnote citation are drawn for the most part from the journals of Captain Cook or his companions. The burden of footnotes is otherwise large, and in these instances I believe the context usually identifies the quotation with the name of the individual from whose journal it comes.

Acknowledgment is made to the Friends of the University of Iowa Libraries, whose semi-annual publication *Books at Iowa* harbored earlier segments of this essay. Thanks should likewise go to Mrs. Helen W. Tuttle of Princeton University Library who, as Chairman of the Publications Committee of Beta Phi Mu, gave generously of her time in handling arrangements for the publication of this present volume in the Chapbook series.

F. P.

I

The First Voyage
1768-1771

OVERLEAF

Engraving of Cook's chart of New Zealand from
volume two of Hawkesworth's *Voyages* (1773).
"Banks's Island" off the eastern coast is in
actuality a peninsula; and the peninsula which
appears on Cook's chart as "Cape South"
is more accurately delineated on modern maps
as Stewart Island. Cook himself later revised
certain of his New Zealand longitudes.

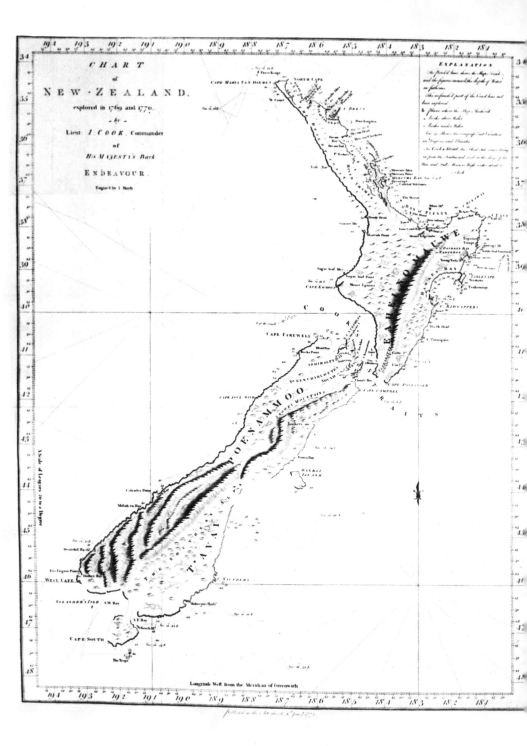

CHART
of
NEW-ZEALAND,
explored in 1769 and 1770.
- by -
Lieut. J. COOK, Commander
of
His MAJESTY'S Bark
ENDEAVOUR.

Engrav'd by I. Bayly

EXPLANATION

Longitude West from the Meridian of Greenwich

TWICE in the 1760's occurred a rare astronomical event which has been observed only five times in history and which will not occur at all in the twentieth century. This is the passage of the planet Venus across the face of the Sun. Until recent years the observation of this transit of Venus was important as furnishing a method of determining the fundamental astronomical unit, namely the Earth's mean distance from the Sun.

With the development of radar reflection techniques and the use of artificial satellites in solar orbit, it appears unlikely that the transits of the twenty-first century will be observed for this purpose. But it is not at all surprising that in the eighteenth century, as in the nineteenth, governments and scientific societies made careful plans to observe the transits of Venus from widely scattered points around the world. At least 151 observers at 77 stations observed the transit which occurred on June 3rd, 1769.[1] It was this transit which occasioned the expeditions of Peter Simon Pallas to Siberia, of the Viennese Jesuit, Father Maximilian Hell, to Lapland, and of Captain Cook to Tahiti.

In June of 1766 the Royal Society of London began making plans for its observation of the forthcoming transit. Two of

1. Harry Woolf, *The Transits of Venus: A Study of Eighteenth-Century Science* (Princeton, 1959), p. 189.

3

the observers selected by the Society were Charles Mason and Jeremiah Dixon, who had recently returned from the North American colonies, where they had surveyed the disputed boundary between Maryland and Pennsylvania, their "Mason and Dixon line" eventually becoming known as the division between the slave states and the free states. Mason was to go to County Donegal in northwest Ireland for his observations of the transit, and Dixon to the island of Hammerfest, off the Norwegian coast. William Wales, who was later to teach mathematics at Christ's Hospital (where the pupils during his time included Samuel Taylor Coleridge, Charles Lamb, and Leigh Hunt), was to make his observations at Hudson's Bay; and the Society recommended that Alexander Dalrymple, a Fellow of the Society and an assiduous collector of charts and accounts of earlier voyages in the South Pacific, be sent to the island of Tahiti, which had recently been discovered by Captain Wallis in the *Dolphin*.

Dalrymple [2] was a foremost proponent of the theory that an enormous land mass—the vaguely located *Terra Australis Incognita* of certain old charts—was yet to be discovered in the South Sea. According to this theory, propounded by Mercator and others, such a continent *must* exist in the south in order to balance the known continents of the north. But Dalrymple was not destined to discover such a continent, nor even to sail to Tahiti. He insisted that he would make the voyage only if he were put in command of the expedition, and this the Lords

2. Dalrymple's relations with Cook are freshly examined in Howard T. Fry, *Alexander Dalrymple and the Expansion of British Trade* (London, 1970), esp. chapter 10.

4

of the Admiralty refused to do on the ground that only an officer of the King's Navy should command a King's ship. Command of the expedition to Tahiti was given to a thirty-nine-year-old warrant officer named James Cook.

Cook had come to the favorable attention of the Admiralty through his superb work as a marine surveyor in North America. In addition to preparing detailed charts of the St. Lawrence River, he had during the past few years charted the coasts and principal harbors of Nova Scotia, Labrador, and Newfoundland.[3] His observation of a solar eclipse in 1766, for the purpose of determining the longitude of Newfoundland, had been communicated to the Royal Society and published in its *Transactions*, and so he was not unknown to that scientific organization. Upon the rejection of the Society's first nominee, Dalrymple, James Cook, and Charles Green, a sometime assistant to the Astronomer Royal, were accepted as the Society's official observers, at Tahiti, of the forthcoming transit of Venus. Cook was promoted to lieutenant and in May of 1768 took command of his designated ship, the bark *Endeavour*, a converted coal-carrier of 366½ tons.

Among his crew of seventy or so were five men who had served under him in Newfoundland, two men, John Gore and Charles Clerke, who had sailed round the world with Commodore Byron, and four (including Gore) who had been with

---

3. Cook's early work as a marine surveyor is bibliographed by R. A. Skelton and R. V. Tooley, "The Marine Surveys of James Cook in North America, 1758-1768," *Map Collectors' Series*, Vol. 4, No. 37 (1967). A facsimile edition of Cook's charts of Newfoundland has been published under the title *James Cook, Surveyor of Newfoundland* (San Francisco, 1965). See also T. M. Knight, "Cook the Cartographer," *Cartography*, Vol. 7, No. 3 (June 1971), pp. 110-118.

the *Dolphin* in her recent circumnavigation. There were also thirteen marines and an apparently satisfactory cook who had lost his right hand. To crowd the accommodations to the utmost, Lieutenant Cook was advised that he was also to receive on board for the voyage a certain Joseph Banks and his party of eight.

Joseph Banks in 1768 was a remarkable young man of twenty-five. Wealthy and insatiably inquisitive, he had a passion for botany which he shared with such older friends as Thomas Pennant, Gilbert White, and Daines Barrington. He was a correspondent of the great Swedish naturalist Linnaeus and a fishing companion of the first Lord of the Admiralty, the fourth Earl of Sandwich. He was later to become an adviser to King George III and to serve as president of the Royal Society for the unprecedented term of forty-two years.[4]

In Banks's entourage, along with two colored servants and two footmen from his country estate, were two artists and two naturalists. These included the very capable Daniel Solander, who had studied under Linnaeus and was later to become Keeper of the Natural History Department of the British Museum. Dr. Solander was to do most of the work of identifying, classifying, and naming the many new plants and animals that were discovered on the voyage. The most active of the artists was Sydney Parkinson, a young man of twenty-three

4. His career is interestingly surveyed by Hector C. Cameron in *Sir Joseph Banks, K.B., P.R.S., The Autocrat of the Philosophers* (London, 1952). Banks's diary of his trip to Labrador, which preceded Cook's first voyage, is now available in an admirable edition by Averil M. Lysaght: *Joseph Banks in Newfoundland and Labrador, 1766: His Diary, Manuscripts and Collections* (Berkeley, 1971).

who had previously exhibited flower paintings at the Society of Arts exhibitions in 1765 and 1766. During the voyage of the *Endeavour* he was to make more than 900 pencil sketches and water-color drawings of plants, birds, reptiles, fishes, and invertebrates, some of them of exquisite workmanship.[5]

5. For a brief note on Parkinson's work, see F. C. Sawyer, "Some Natural History Drawings Made During Captain Cook's First Voyage Round the World," *Journal of the Society for the Bibliography of Natural History*, Vol. 2, Pt. 6 (October, 1950), pp. 190-193.

THE FIRST VOYAGE

1768-1771

⚓

LEAVING Plymouth Harbour on August 26, 1768, the *Endeavour* stopped at Madeira to take on fresh water, a large supply of onions, and some 3,000 gallons of wine, and then sailed for South America. Toward the middle of November the ship was off the coast of Brazil, but much to the annoyance of Cook and his men they were refused permission by the Portuguese governor to disembark at Rio de Janeiro. Nonetheless they were able to purchase fresh fruit, meat, and vegetables, and while they lay at anchor Joseph Banks managed to slip ashore to botanize, Sydney Parkinson made twenty-two drawings of Brazilian fishes, and Cook drew a plan of the harbor. Christmas Day and New Year's came and went as they sailed southward, and in mid-January they reached the eastern tip of Tierra del Fuego. In this unlikely spot (not to be botanized again till 1832, when Charles Darwin touched there in the *Beagle*) Banks, Solander, and a party went ashore and were caught overnight in a midsummer snowstorm. By morning, Banks's two Negro servants had frozen to death.

The passage around Cape Horn was remarkably smooth and in early April they reached Tahiti in good time to set up an observatory and tents and surround the spot with an earthenwork enclosure which they named Fort Venus. Despite this precaution and the presence of sentries, the light-fingered natives made off with the astronomical quadrant, but the instrument was recovered by Banks and repaired by the astronomer Green. June 3, 1769, was a bright and cloudless day at Tahiti, and the transit of Venus was independently observed by Cook, Green, and Solander.[6] A three-month stay at this beautiful island gave Cook time to chart the coasts in detail and overhaul the ship while Banks collected birds and plants and made shrewd inquiries into the customs of the friendly natives. Two marines who tried to desert were brought back on board, a native priest named Tupia and his servant-boy Tayeto were embarked, and on July 13th the *Endeavour* sailed westward to the neighboring islands of Huahine, Raiatea, and Bora-Bora, which Cook surveyed and plotted on his charts.

Cook's instructions[7] now required him to plunge southward 1500 miles to search for the mythical southern continent, which he was to chart and take possession of "in the name of the King of Great Britain." Should he fail to find such a continent, he was to sail westward to the land (New Zealand) which the Dutch navigator Abel Tasman had touched upon in 1642. On European charts, New Zealand was only a line which might possibly, it was thought, be the western edge of the great unknown continent. For over six weeks the *Endeavour* sailed to the south with no sign of the continent and then,

6. "Every wished-for favourable circumstance attended the whole of that day, without one single impediment, excepting the heat, which was intolerable," Cook reported. "The thermometer which hung by the clock and was exposed to the sun as we were, was at one time as high as 119°." For Cook's report to the Royal Society on November 21, 1771, see *Philosophical Transactions of the Royal Society*, Vol. 61 (1771), pp. 397-436.

7. Cook's secret instructions were first printed in the *Publications of the Navy Records Society*, Vol. 63 (1928), pp. 343ff.

with increasingly bad weather, turned westward toward New Zealand. Land was sighted on October 6, and Banks optimistically recorded that "all hands seem to agree that this is certainly the Continent we are in search of." The natives proved exceedingly hostile, but Tupia the Polynesian found that he could understand the language and make himself understood.[8]

Ten days were spent at Mercury Bay, where Charles Green observed a transit of Mercury, and the charting of the coast continued as Cook rounded the northern tip of New Zealand, fixed the position of Cape Maria van Diemen despite hurricanes and high seas, and in mid-January, 1770, put into Queen Charlotte's Sound to repair the ship. Here the natives were friendly, though from the presence of human bones near their campfires it was clear that they were cannibals. The naturalists saw none of the flightless birds of New Zealand, such as the kiwi, but Banks did hear the bell-birds and noted that "their voices were certainly the most melodious wild music I have ever heard, almost imitating small bells but with the most tuneable silver sound imaginable."

Having made a circuit of the northern island of New Zealand, Cook next sailed round the southern island, "to the total demolition of our aerial fabric called continent." In something over six months he circumnavigated both islands and charted them with such precision that his map of New Zealand has

8. Cook's first landing in New Zealand is recounted in detail by W. L. Williams, "On the Visit of Captain Cook to Poverty Bay and Tolaga Bay," *Transactions and Proceedings of the New Zealand Institute,* Vol. 21 (1888), pp. 389-397. See also J. A. Mackay, *Historic Poverty Bay,* 2nd ed. (Gisborne, N.Z., 1966), pp. 16-62. A more general work, lavishly illustrated, is A. Charles Begg and Neil C. Begg, *James Cook and New Zealand* (Wellington, N.Z., 1969).

been called one of the major achievements of the eighteenth century.[9]

Having carried out his instructions, Cook decided, in council with his officers, to return to England by way of the East Indies. A return in high latitudes by way of Cape Horn might have permitted him to dispel the continental theory conclusively, since a large area of the South Pacific between 40° and 60° S. remained untraversed. Cook himself favored this Horn route, but the southern winter was approaching, and so on the first of April, 1770, the *Endeavour* left New Zealand and sailed westward. Cook's intention was to reach the unexplored eastern coast of Australia and follow it northward to New Guinea.

On April 19 the coast of Australia was sighted, and ten days later a landing was made to take on fresh water. The exotic birds, wild flowers and gum trees were a delight to the botanists, and the abundance of large sting-rays in the bay at first impelled Cook to call this spot Sting-ray Harbour, a name he later changed to Botany Bay. (Botany Bay was later to become the site of the first British colony in the Pacific.) So numerous were the botanical acquisitions that the artist Sydney Parkinson was overwhelmed with work, although within fourteen days he made ninety-four sketches. Pelicans nearly five feet high were seen farther north, and in a mangrove swamp Banks found a species of green ants. Sailing near the coast, charting as he went, Cook unawares approached the Great Barrier Reef, and on a calm moonlit night, though soundings were

9. It is so characterized by J. C. Beaglehole, *The Exploration of the Pacific*, 3rd ed. (London, 1966), p. 244.

continually being made, the *Endeavour* struck and grounded on the coral rocks.

Hoping to get his ship off at the next high tide, Cook jettisoned some forty or fifty tons of ballast and supplies,[10] but the mid-morning tide was insufficient, and the leaks increased. Three pumps were manned, "at which every man on board assisted, the Captain, Mr. Banks, and all the officers, not excepted." With great good luck the sea remained calm and at high tide the next night, after twenty-three hours on the rocks, the ship floated free. A narrow river some thirty miles distant was found where the ship could be beached and repaired.

Seven weeks at the Endeavour River allowed Banks and Solander time to hunt and botanize and to attempt some contact with the natives. One of the men reported seeing a winged animal "about the size of, and much like, a one gallon cagg" (probably a flying fox) and John Gore became the first Englishman to shoot a kangaroo. The natives were a shy, naked, chocolate-brown race whose language differed from the Polynesian and Maori tongues. On August 6 the *Endeavour* was able to put to sea, though not before the natives, angry because they were not allowed to carry off a turtle from aboard the ship, had set fire to the grass surrounding Cook's campsite.

With difficulty Cook maneuvered his ship through the reef to the open sea, but this course proved even more dangerous

---

10. In 1969, after they had lain under the sea for 199 years, six cannon from the *Endeavour*, along with two cannon balls and pieces of iron and stone ballast, were recovered by an American expedition from the Philadelphia Academy of Science. Details of the restoration are given in C. Pearson, "The Preservation of Iron Cannon after 200 Years under the Sea," *Studies in Conservation*, Vol. 17, No. 3 (August 1972), pp. 91-110.

than the treacherous navigation closer in, for the trade wind and the tide drove the ship toward huge breakers smashing against the rocks. Providentially, at the moment of greatest peril, an opening in the reef appeared, and the *Endeavour* hurried through and once again sailed along the coast inside the Great Barrier Reef. Two weeks of cautious sailing brought the ship to the Torres Strait, and Cook was able to confirm the existence of a sea passage between Australia and New Guinea. He had charted, during the past four months, nearly 2,000 miles of the hitherto-unknown coast of Eastern Australia.

Sailing again in known waters, the *Endeavour*, early in October, reached Batavia (Jakarta) in Java. Here the ship was repaired by skillful Dutch shipwrights. Hitherto the men had been in good health, thanks to Cook's insistence on cleanliness and his unremitting attention to proper diet, and no one on his ship had succumbed to scurvy. But Batavia at that time was a pestilential port, and before the *Endeavour* could leave in late December, seven of her people had died, including the two Polynesians, Tupia and Tayeto, and many others were ill from malaria or dysentery. Before the ship reached the Cape of Good Hope in March, twenty-two more had died, among them the astronomer Charles Green and the artist Sydney Parkinson. After a voyage of nearly three years, Cook brought the *Endeavour* back to England and anchored in the Downs on July 13, 1771.

Upon the recommendation of David Garrick, Dr. Charles Burney, and perhaps other friends of Lord Sandwich, a writer named John Hawkesworth was chosen to edit the official account of Cook's first voyage. Hawkesworth was an early

associate of Dr. Samuel Johnson and a writer of essays, reviews, poems, and oratorios.[11] His scientific qualifications for
this particular undertaking were meager, but he produced a
readable work by conflating or dovetailing the separate journals kept by Cook and Banks. The work was eagerly awaited
and appeared in 1773 as volumes two and three of a three-
volume set entitled *An Account of the Voyages undertaken
by the Order of His Present Majesty for making Discoveries
in the Southern Hemisphere, and successively performed by
Commodore Byron, Captain Wallis, Captain Carteret, and
Captain Cook, in the Dolphin, the Swallow, and the Endeavour: drawn up from the Journals which were kept by the several Commanders, and from the Papers of Joseph Banks, Esq.
. . . Illustrated with Cuts, and a great Variety of Charts and
Maps relative to Countries now first discovered, or hitherto
but imperfectly known.*

These volumes were widely read, but Hawkesworth became the target of severe criticism, chiefly because he included
descriptions of some of the more erotic native customs and
because he did not attribute some of the lucky escapes of the
voyagers to the particular interposition of Providence. The
£6000 which he received for his editorial work was perhaps
small recompense for the ignominy which unfairly overtook
him. Hawkesworth's alleged suicide is unproved, but un-
doubtedly his reputation was in eclipse after the publication of

---

11. As yet no book-length study of Hawkesworth has been published, though
a step in this direction has been made in Robert E. Gallagher's unpublished
Northwestern University doctoral dissertation, *John Hawkesworth: A Study
Toward a Literary Biography* (1957).

his book of voyages. "The severe reception it encountered, the suspicion of infidelity set on foot, and, above all, the strange fact of a lax magazine culling from it all the warmest passages to make a new art of love, preyed on his spirits, and drove him also to suicide." [12]

For 120 years it was through Hawkesworth's compilation that Cook's first voyage was known to the public. Not until 1893 did an edition of Cook's original journal appear. In that year Captain (later Admiral) W. J. L. Wharton, Hydrographer of the Admiralty, published an edition based upon a manuscript copy of Cook's journal now owned by the Mitchell Library, Sydney. [13] No copy of the journal in Cook's own handwriting was then known to exist, but in 1923 such a holograph journal was sold at auction and is now in the possession of the Commonwealth National Library, Canberra. It is this manuscript which furnished the basis of the now-standard text, edited with full apparatus by Professor J. C. Beaglehole and published in 1955 for the Hakluyt Society. [14]

There was no separate publication of Joseph Banks's journal until 1896, when Sir Joseph Dalton Hooker, eminent botanist, explorer, and lifelong friend of Charles Darwin, published a ruthlessly abridged version [15] based on a transcript of a nine-

12. Percy Fitzgerald, *The Life of David Garrick*, rev. ed. (London, 1899), p. 196.
13. W. J. L. Wharton, ed., *Captain Cook's Journal during his First Voyage Round the World made in H. M. Bark "Endeavour" 1768-71 ...* (London, 1893).
14. J. C. Beaglehole, ed., *The Journals of Captain James Cook on His Voyages of Discovery*, Vol. 1: *The Voyage of the* Endeavour, *1768-71* (Cambridge, 1955).
15. Joseph D. Hooker, ed., *Journal of the Right Hon. Sir Joseph Banks, Bart., K.B., P.R.S., during Captain Cook's First Voyage in H.M.S. Endeavour in 1768-71...* (London, 1896).

teenth-century copy, Banks's original manuscript journal being then in private hands and unavailable. In 1958 the New
Zealand pages of Banks's journal, edited from an eighteenth-
century transcript now in the Alexander Turnbull Library,
Wellington, were separately published,[16] and finally in 1962
appeared a splendid two-volume edition of the entire journal,[17]
printed from Banks's original manuscript in the Mitchell Library, Sydney, and embellished with many of Sydney Parkinson's botanical drawings, some of which are reproduced in
color.

Hawkesworth's compilation had included (without credit)
engravings of some of Sydney Parkinson's drawings, and
Parkinson's brother Stansfield was able to include some two
dozen drawings in the edition of Sydney Parkinson's journal
which appeared in 1773 under the title *A Journal of a Voyage
to the South Seas, in his Majesty's Ship, the Endeavour. . . .*,
but most of the Parkinson drawings were owned by Joseph
Banks. Banks apparently planned to publish these in a sump-
tuous folio work with a text by Daniel Solander. Copperplate
engravings of several hundred of the botanical and zoological
drawings were actually prepared, and Daniel Solander's careful descriptions were largely completed, but following Solander's death in 1782 Banks lost interest in the projected work
and it has never been published.[18] In the Botanical Department

16. William P. Morrell, ed., *Sir Joseph Banks in New Zealand* (Wellington,
1958).

17. J. C. Beaglehole, ed., *The* Endeavour *Journal of Joseph Banks 1768-1771*,
2 vols. (Sydney, 1962).

18. The engravings of the plants collected in Australia, with Solander's notes
in Latin, were published by the British Museum (Natural History) in three

of the British Museum (Natural History) at South Kensington repose hundreds of Parkinson's original drawings, the engraved plates and proof impressions, together with Solander's voluminous notes. Solander had hoped to publish a survey of natural history "comparable to that of Linné's *Systema Naturae*, but on an even more extensive and accurate scale than Gmelin's edition as well as more replete with personal knowledge." [19] But today Solander is remembered, if he is remembered at all, as the inventor of the Solander case, a type of box sometimes used to protect rare books, which he devised to hold his notes. [20]

---

volumes between 1901 and 1905. See *Illustrations of Australian Plants Collected in 1770 During Captain Cook's Voyage round the World in H.M.S.* Endeavour *by The Right Hon. Sir Joseph Banks, Bart., K.B., P.R.S., and Dr. Daniel Solander, F. R. S. . . . With Determinations by James Britten, F.L.S.* For a concise survey of the botanical work, see William F. Stearn, "The Botanical Results of the *Endeavour* Voyage," *Endeavour*, Vol. 27, No. 100 (January 1968), pp. 3-10. This may be supplemented by E. W. Groves, "Notes on the Botanical Specimens Collected by Banks and Solander on Cook's First Voyage, together with an Itinerary of Landing Localities," *Journal of the Society for the Bibliography of Natural History*, Vol. 4, Pt. 1 (January 1962), pp. 57-62.

19. Tom Iredale, "Solander as a Conchologist," *Proceedings of the Malacological Society of London*, Vol. 12 (1916), p. 86.

20. Solander has recently become the subject of a monograph by Roy Anthony Rauschenberg, "Daniel Carl Solander, Naturalist on the 'Endeavour,'" *Transactions of the American Philosophical Society*, n.s., Vol. 58, Pt. 8 (1968).

II

The Second Voyage

1772-1775

OVERLEAF

Chart of the Southern Hemisphere from volume
one of Captain Cook's *A Voyage Towards the
South Pole and Round the World* (1777).
A portrait painted by Nathaniel Dance in 1776
shows Cook holding a copy of this polar
zenithal map of the second voyage.

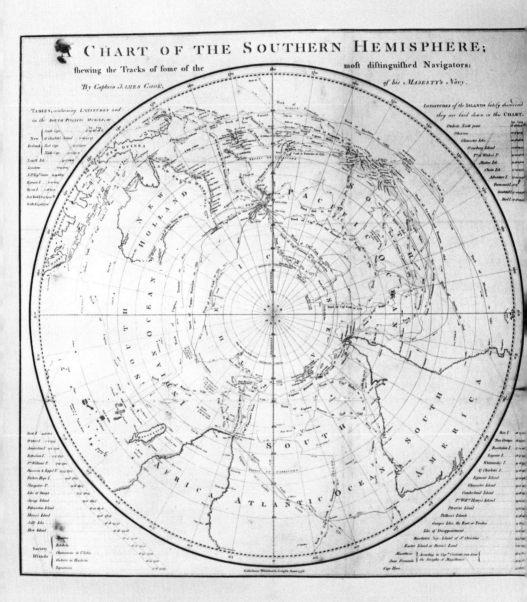

A CHART OF THE SOUTHERN HEMISPHERE;

shewing the Tracks of some of the most distinguished Navigators:

By Captain JAMES COOK. of his MAJESTY's Navy.

IN 1770 Alexander Dalrymple flamboyantly dedicated the first volume of his *Historical Collection of the Several Voyages and Discoveries in the South Pacific Ocean* "To the man who, emulous of Magellan and the heroes of former times, . . . shall . . . succeed in establishing an intercourse with a Southern Continent." The legend of a great Southern continent had persisted through the centuries, and Cook's first voyage, completed in 1771, did not wholly dispel the ancient legend.[1] In a postscript to his journal of the first voyage, Cook suggested the best course to pursue in making further discoveries in the South Sea. His plan was adopted by the Admiralty, and within three months of his return, orders had been given for the purchase and fitting out of two new ships for a second voyage of exploration. The *Resolution*, a sloop of 462 tons and a complement of 112 men, was to be commanded by James Cook, and a consort ship, the *Adventure*, of 340 tons with some 80 men was placed under the command of Tobias Furneaux, who had

1. "The story of the origin and persistence of the belief in that continent, of the controversies which grew out of that belief, of the centuries of exploration in search of the elusive shores of the Terra Australis, is one of the most curiously interesting in the record of human thought and action." See Lawrence C. Wroth, "The Early Cartography of the Pacific," *The Papers of the Bibliographical Society of America*, Vol. 38, No. 2 (Second Quarter, 1944), esp. pp. 163-179.

sailed with Wallis in the *Dolphin*.[2] The *Resolution* was given a new upper deck and a roundhouse, to make room for Joseph Banks and his dozen scientists, artists, horn players, and assistants; but with these alterations the ship became so top heavy that it was found necessary to restore the *Resolution* to her original condition. At this thwarting of his wishes, Banks withdrew in anger, chartered a ship of his own, and took his retinue on a trip to Iceland instead.[3]

As a replacement for Daniel Solander and James Lind, the scientists whom Banks had secured to accompany Cook's second expedition, the Admiralty chose John Reinhold Forster, an erudite but quarrelsome German scholar. Forster, adept at languages, had translated numerous travel books into English, among them Kalm's *Travels into North America* (1770-71), Osbeck's *A Voyage to China and the East Indies* (1771), and Bougainville's *A Voyage Round the World* (1772). He had also published a monograph on mineralogy, a catalog of British insects, and catalogs of North American plants and animals. For the Royal Society he had prepared descriptions of bird and fish specimens from the Hudson's Bay area, and his articles on natural history had appeared in the Society's *Philosophical Transactions*. It was Forster's expectation that he would write an account of this present voyage.

J. R. Forster's seventeen-year-old son George accompanied his father on the *Resolution*. George had shown considerable talent in drawing, and during the voyage he was to make many

2. For details of his career see Rupert Furneaux, *Tobias Furneaux, Circumnavigator* (London, 1960).

3. See Halldór Hermannsson, *Sir Joseph Banks and Iceland* (Ithaca, N.Y., 1928).

workmanlike sketches of plants, fishes, birds, and insects. This voyage with Cook proved to be a stimulating time for George. He later returned to Germany, married Teresa Heyne, daughter of contemporary Europe's leading classical scholar, Christian Heyne of Göttingen, taught at several universities, and served as librarian to the Elector of Mainz. A trip down the Rhine and to England in 1790 with Alexander von Humboldt gave rise to his most highly-regarded book, *Ansichten vom Niederrhein* (*Views from the Lower Rhine*). His annual reviews of English literature, his essays on geography, natural history and politics, his translations, his letters, and his many-sided contacts with the world of his time have led to his characterization as "one of the most fascinating figures in the field of Anglo-German literary relations in the eighteenth century."[4] At the end, his radical political views entangled him in the French Revolution, he was reviled by his father and his friends, deserted by his wife, and at the height of the Terror he died in Paris at the age of thirty-nine. He can be seen briefly, stumbling over a cannonball, in Thomas Carlyle's *The French Revolution.*[5]

Joseph Banks had expected to take four artists along with

4. W. D. Robson-Scott, "Georg Forster and the Gothic Revival," *The Modern Language Review*, Vol. 51, No. 1 (January 1956), p. 42.

5. For a brief but sound survey of George Forster's career, see the article by Robert L. Kahn in Stanley Kunitz and Vineta Colby, eds., *European Authors, 1000-1900* (New York, 1967), pp. 290-291. At present the best discussion in English of Forster's later career is Leslie Bodi, "Georg Forster: The 'Pacific Expert' of Eighteenth-century Germany," *Historical Studies, Australia and New Zealand*, Vol. 8, No. 32 (May 1959), pp. 345-363. For an entrance into the voluminous German literature, see Kurt Kersten, *Der Weltumsegler: Johann Georg Adam Forster, 1754-1794* (Bern, 1957). In recent years George Forster has become the subject of two or three novels published in East Germany.

him on Cook's second voyage: John Zoffany, a portrait painter; John Cleveley, a marine painter; and John and James Miller, natural-history draftsmen. After Banks abandoned his plan to accompany the voyage, the Admiralty settled upon William Hodges as the official artist. Hodges was a twenty-eight-year-old landscape painter who had studied under Richard Wilson. He had previously painted scenery for a theatre in Derby and had exhibited views at the Society of Artists exhibitions. During the second voyage he worked industriously with oils, chalks, crayons, washes, and pen (Cook admiringly called him "indefatigable"), and many of his oil paintings are today still in the possession of the Admiralty. After his return from his voyage with Cook, Hodges spent six years in India, where he enjoyed the friendship and patronage of Warren Hastings.[6] Although Sir Joshua Reynolds considered him "a very intelligent and ingenious artist," Hodges' rendering of atmosphere and light noticeably affected his technique, and one of his early critics complained that his paintings appear "as if the colours were laid on the canvas with a skewer."[7] His handling of sylvan scenes can be examined in the two illustrations he prepared for Boydell's famous Shakespeare Gallery: a view of Portia's garden in *The Merchant of Venice* (V, i) and the Forest of Arden in *As You Like It* (II, i).

6. Details of his later career are brought together by William Foster, "William Hodges, R.A., in India," *Bengal: Past and Present* [Journal of the Calcutta Historical Society], Vol. 30 (July-December 1925), pp. 1-8. From Hodges' sojourn in India came a portfolio of forty-five color plates, *Select Views in India* (1786-88), and a book entitled *Travels in India* (1793).

7. The technique of Hodges' work during Cook's second voyage is discussed in detail by Bernard Smith, *European Vision and the South Pacific, 1768-1850: A Study in the History of Art and Ideas* (Oxford, 1960), esp. pp. 39-58.

In addition to a natural scientist and an official artist, both appointed by the Admiralty, Cook had with him on the *Resolution* an official astronomer, William Wales, appointed by the Board of Longitude. Determining the position of a ship at sea was still a difficult problem in the mid-eighteenth century. On his first voyage, Cook had relied upon the method of "lunar distances" to find his longitude. This required him to observe the distance of the Moon from the Sun or from certain fixed stars and then to compare this observed distance with the distances which had previously been tabulated at the Royal Observatory in Greenwich. (Tables were available in the new *Nautical Almanac and Astronomical Ephemeris*, which had first been prepared for the year 1767 by Nevil Maskelyne, Astronomer Royal.) From such calculations he could determine the difference between Greenwich time and local time and thereby ascertain his longitude. To achieve tolerable accuracy, corrections for refraction, parallax and other distortions had to be made, and it could require up to four hours to complete the necessary mathematical computations. Cook was sufficiently skillful that he was often able to find his longitude to within one degree or better by this lunar method. But the Board of Longitude was seeking a simpler method, and on his second voyage Cook carried with him four experimental timepieces. Since knowledge of a standard time is a crucial factor in determining longitude, it may seem surprising that marine chronometers had not yet come into use. The difficulty was to construct a timepiece which would be unaffected by extremes of temperature and capable of keeping accurate time in a rolling and pitching ship. The two timepieces in the *Resolution* were put in the care of William Wales. During the voyage the watch constructed by John Arnold (it was one of his early models) performed erratically and finally stopped; the model built by Larcum Kendall to the specifications of John Harrison worked to Cook's satisfaction and demonstrated that longitude at sea could be found accurately by means of a chronometer.[8] Until the 1920's when the broadcasting of radio time signals became possible, ocean-going vessels relied upon chronometers keeping Greenwich mean time to determine the ship's longitude.

8. The construction of an accurate marine timekeeper has been called "one of the most intricate and difficult mechanical problems which Man has ever been called upon to solve." Rupert T. Gould, "John Harrison and His Timekeepers," *The Mariner's Mirror* (April 1935), p. 121. For details and photographs of Cook's marine timekeepers and of the pendulum clocks used by his astronomers, see Derek Howse and Beresford Hutchinson, *The Clocks and Watches of Captain James Cook, 1769-1969*, reprinted from the four quarterly issues, 1969, of *Antiquarian Horology*.

THE SECOND VOYAGE

1772-1775

⚓

THE *Resolution* and the *Adventure* sailed from Plymouth on July 13, 1772, and headed for Capetown, South Africa, which was to be their point of departure into the cold and uncharted southern waters. The usual stop at Madeira to take on wine and onions, which Cook valued as an antiscorbutic, was followed by a less usual stop for water at Santiago in the Cape Verde Islands. Sailing south for seventy-seven days, the ships had pleasant weather, and on the 29th of October they sighted the Cape of Good Hope. From the deck of the *Resolution*, anchored in Table Bay, Hodges painted a large view of Capetown "of astonishing vigor and originality" which Cook immediately arranged to send back to England.[9]

During the next three weeks, while the ships were being recaulked, the Forsters, father and son, made excursions around the town and up to Table Mountain. The elder Forster collected some fine specimens of insects, and he sent back to the Royal Society several red bishop-birds, four curlew sandpipers, and a black korhaan bird. Francis Masson, a botanist who had taken passage out on the *Resolution* to collect South

9. Now in the possession of the National Maritime Museum, this painting hung for over a century and a half in the house of the First Lord of the Admiralty. It is reproduced, together with a modern photograph of the same view, in Geoffrey Callender, " 'Cape Town' by William Hodges, R.A.," *The Burlington Magazine*, Vol. 79 (September 1941), p. 95.

African plants and bulbs for the Royal Gardens at Kew, left the ship's company at Capetown; and possibly to help fill this void in their scientific companionship the Forsters persuaded Cook to let them hire, as an assistant naturalist, a young Swedish botanist named Anders Sparrman. Although at this time he was only twenty-four years old, Sparrman had already made a voyage to China as surgeon in a Swedish East Indiaman. He was now in Capetown studying the flora. Another change in personnel, necessitated by an illness in Furneaux's ship, was the transfer of James Burney from the *Resolution* to the *Adventure*. This was a promotion for Burney, and it greatly pleased his young sister, the novelist Fanny Burney, to learn that Cook had made him a lieutenant.[10]

On 22 November the two ships sailed southward and began a search for the promontory ("Cape Circumcision") which a Frenchman, Bouvet, had reported seeing on New Year's Day in 1739. Bouvet's view had been obscured by fogs, but he believed that he had sighted a part of the Great Southern Continent. Fogs began to envelop Cook's ships too. The temperature dropped rapidly, early in December snow began falling, and the casks of drinking water on deck started to freeze. Icebergs soon appeared, sixty feet high, white or crystal clear, beautiful sometimes as they reflected the blue and green of the sea or the gold of the sun, but forming a treacherous gauntlet through which the ships had to make their way. It was just such a scene that William Wales's future pupil Samuel Taylor

10. See G. E. Manwaring, *My Friend the Admiral: The Life, Letters, and Journals of Rear-Admiral James Burney, F.R.S., The Companion of Captain Cook and Friend of Charles Lamb* (London, 1931), p. 20.

Coleridge was to describe in the enchanted lines of *The Ancient Mariner:*

> And now there came both mist and snow,
> And it grew wondrous cold;
> And ice mast high came floating by,
> As green as emerald.[11]

Unable to find land where Bouvet claimed to have seen it, Cook concluded that what the Frenchman had seen was an iceberg. He did not know that Bouvet's reported longitude was seven degrees in error and that his predecessor had in fact seen a small oval island, one of the most remote spots of land on the globe.

On Christmas Day the sailors caroused and held boxing matches on the windswept deck. The scientists fought the tedium of monotonous days by examining and describing the oceanic birds, whale birds, albatrosses, blue and silver-grey petrels, making the first comprehensive record of the birds of the sub-Antarctic. Out alone in the jolly boat one calm day, hunting birds and testing the temperature of the sea at various depths, Wales and the elder Forster found themselves lost in the fog for an unnerving time, beyond sight and sound of the

11. It has been asserted that "no other voyage in the whole realm of travel literature affords so many parallels with the voyage of the Ancient Mariner as does Cook's second voyage." Bernard Smith, "Coleridge's *Ancient Mariner* and Cook's Second Voyage," *Journal of the Warburg and Courtauld Institutes,* Vol. 19 (January-June 1956), p. 150. Cook's comments on ice conditions are studied in the light of present-day knowledge by H.F.P. Herdman, "Some Notes on Sea Ice Observed by Captain James Cook, R.N., During His Circumnavigation of Antarctica, 1772-75," *The Journal of Glaciology,* Vol. 3, No. 26 (October 1959), pp. 534-541.

ships. Finally the ringing of a dinner bell on the *Adventure* guided them back to safety. After crossing the Antarctic Circle southwest of Enderby Land on January 17, 1773, the first ships in history to sail so far south, the *Resolution* and the *Adventure* were parted by fog. Furneaux and Cook fired cannons every half hour but could hear no answer, and after two days they proceeded on separate courses. Foreseeing such a contingency, Cook had stipulated that the two ships should rendezvous at Queen Charlotte's Sound in New Zealand.

The *Adventure* landed first in Tasmania. James Burney drew a chart of the southeast coast, showing the track of the ship, and a chart of Adventure Bay. Both ships, in mid-February, had seen the Southern Lights and made the first recorded observations of these auroras of the southern hemisphere. In late March the *Resolution* reached the southwestern tip of New Zealand and entered Dusky Bay after being out of sight of land for 122 days. In this primeval spot "which must surely have been dozing from the day of its creation until now" Cook found a plentiful supply of fish and ducks, and he remained here six weeks. Hodges made paintings of a waterfall and of a family of natives, George Forster drew sketches of fish and birds, Wales set up an observatory, and Cook carefully surveyed and mapped Dusky Bay, with its maze of islands and inlets.[12]

Early in May, his crew refreshed, Cook sailed up to Queen Charlotte's Sound. Off Cape Stephens the ship's company ob-

12. Historical as well as present-day information on Dusky Bay will be found in a well-illustrated volume by A. Charles Begg and Neil C. Begg, *Dusky Bay*, rev. ed. (Christchurch, N.Z., 1968).

served four waterspouts twisting eerily between sea and sky. Hodges rapidly sketched the scene and later portrayed this incident in an oil painting. The *Adventure*, rigged down for winter, had been waiting at the rendezvous since early April. Cook gave orders that scurvy-grass and wild celery, which grew abundantly in the area, should be added to the diet of Furneaux's ailing crew, and on June 7th the ships again put to sea. Still searching for the legendary continent, they ran eastward, halfway to the coast of Chile, before looping northward toward Tahiti. The refreshments of that tropical island were urgently needed to counteract symptoms of scurvy among the crew of the *Adventure;* and so, without taking time to run down its true location, Cook passed through the area where Carteret had seen Pitcairn Island in 1767. Not until the mutineers from the *Bounty* landed there in 1790 was Pitcairn Island explored.

In mid-August the peaks of Tahiti rose invitingly against a brilliant sky, but quirks of wind and tide nearly wrecked both ships on the surrounding reefs before a safe anchorage was made. The strain was beginning to affect Cook's health. Two weeks at Tahiti, however, with its fresh fruits and delightful climate, greatly restored the ships' companies, and at Huahine, a neighboring island where the ships stopped for a few September days, fowls and hogs were obtained in abundant supply. Apparently envious of his black silk waistcoat, two natives at Huahine attacked and disrobed Anders Sparrman, who had incautiously wandered off alone searching for botanical specimens. "The worthy Sparrman," a later writer surmised, "stalked forth from the bush wearing only his spectacles." It was here that Captain Furneaux took aboard Omai, one of the natives, who subsequently sailed with the *Adventure* to England. Omai was to become, for a season, a lion of fashionable London society.[13]

Trending southwestward on a course back to New Zealand, Cook discovered Hervey Island (Manuae), an atoll in the group now known as the Cook Islands, and he surveyed the islands of Eua and Tongatapu. Bright red feathers obtained here from the islanders proved valuable as an article of trade elsewhere. Among the curiosities that Sparrman collected were a tortoise-shell trolling hook with a shank of whalebone and a necklace made of translucent-blue parrot bones.[14]

As the *Resolution* and the *Adventure* neared Cook Straits between the North and South islands of New Zealand, a violent storm began buffeting the two ships, and the gales continued for over a week. On 3 November the *Resolution* came safely to rest at her old anchorage in Queen Charlotte's Sound and waited for the *Adventure* to appear. Cabbages, carrots, onions, and parsley were growing exuberantly in a garden that Furneaux had laid out five months earlier, wild celery and scurvy grass were gathered, and fish were obtained from the natives. (George Forster observed that these natives often wore necklaces of human teeth.) The *Adventure* had not appeared by November 25th; and after coasting round several of

13. See Thomas Blake Clark, *Omai, First Polynesian Ambassador to England* (San Francisco, 1940). The Abbé Baston published a fictitious autobiography of Omai in four volumes, *Narrations d'Omai* (Rouen, 1790), which has sometimes been mistaken for a true account.

14. These and other artifacts are still preserved at Stockholm in the Ethnographical Museum of Sweden. See J. Söderstrom, *A. Sparrman's Ethnographical Collection from James Cook's 2nd Expedition (1772-1775)* (Stockholm, 1939).

the coves firing cannon, Cook gave up hope of meeting with his consort ship, and the *Resolution* sailed off alone to explore the Antarctic waters between New Zealand and Cape Horn.

The *Adventure*, meanwhile, had been blown toward the North island of New Zealand, where she anchored in Tolaga Bay to repair damaged rigging and take on supplies of wood and water. Contrary winds kept her from reaching Queen Charlotte's Sound until the 30th of November, when she discovered that the *Resolution* had departed a few days earlier. By mid-December the *Adventure* too was ready to leave, and one of Furneaux's final preparations was to send out a cutter with ten men to gather a supply of wild greens. When this party failed to return, Furneaux ordered Lieutenant Burney and several marines to take the launch and go in search of them. Near Grass Cove, Burney found some baskets of fresh meat lying on the beach, then some shoes belonging to their men, and then a severed hand. Farther up, natives were clustered around a fire. Dispersing these cannibals with musket shots, Burney found "such a shocking scene of carnage and barbarity as can never be mentioned or thought of but with horror; for the heads, hearts, and lungs of several of our people were seen lying on the beach, and, at a little distance, the dogs gnawing their intrails." On the 23rd or 24th of December, Furneaux managed to get clear of Cook Straits. He sailed past Cape Horn, made another unsuccessful search for Bouvet's Island, and on the 17th of March, 1774, the *Adventure* anchored again at Capetown. Here Furneaux left a letter for Cook telling of the massacre of his boat's crew, and his ship returned to England after an absence of exactly two years.

Two weeks before the *Adventure* sailed from New Zealand, the *Resolution*, steering southeastward, had already seen her first ice. This was apparently a summer of unusually heavy ice in Antarctic waters. Ice coated the sails and festooned the rigging, stiffened the ropes into wires, and made the ship difficult to handle. Snow and sleet and fog drizzled down, though the sun hung above the horizon even at midnight. On December 20th the *Resolution* crossed the Antarctic Circle for a second time and was soon surrounded by massive icebergs. To George Forster's eyes "the whole scene looked like the wrecks of a shattered world, or as the poets describe some regions of hell." Cook hauled to the north for a time, sailed eastward, and again pushed toward the south. Icebergs crowded the ship, one of them towering 200 feet tall, its top looking "not unlike the cupola of St. Paul's church." Occasional whales were seen, while petrels and albatrosses wheeled around the ship. For a third time, on January 26th, 1774, Cook crossed the Antarctic Circle and continued southward for three days, when progress in that direction was halted by an immense field of ice which stretched to the south "looking like a ridge of mountains, rising one above another till they were lost in the clouds." It was Cook's opinion that this ice "extended quite to the pole, or perhaps joined to some land, to which it had been affixed from the earliest time."

I, who had ambition not only to go farther than any one had been before, but as far as it was possible for man to go, was not sorry at meeting with this interruption; as it, in some measure, relieved us; at least, shortened the dangers and hardships inseparable from the navigation of the southern polar regions. Since therefore we could

not proceed one inch farther to the South, no other reason need be
assigned for my tacking, and standing back to the North; being at
this time in the latitude of 71° 10' South, longitude 106° 54' West.

At this position Cook was in the Amundsen Sea off the Wal-
green Coast of Antarctica, perhaps 150 miles from Thurston
Island. No ship was to push farther south in this particular
longitude until February of 1960, when two icebreakers from
the United States Navy bulldozed their way past Thurston
Island.

Morale was high, his crew was in good health, provisions
appeared to be adequate, and so Cook resolved to winter once
again in the tropics and then make a deep exploration of the
South Atlantic Ocean during the following austral summer.
On sailing north and finding no land along the 38th parallel,
where Dalrymple placed the eastern coast of "Juan Fernández
Land," Cook turned to the northwest in order to pinpoint the
location of Easter Island. Tropical birds were seen on the first
of March, and as the weather became warmer symptoms of
scurvy began to appear. Cook himself fell dangerously ill with
a stomach ailment. The ship's surgeon tried opiates and enemas
and plasters and hot baths to quiet Cook's fits of violent hic-
coughing. No other fresh meat being available, J. R. Forster
sacrificed his pet Tahitian dog, which furnished the captain
with a hot broth he was able to keep down, and his strength
began to return.

On March 13th, having been out of sight of land for over a
hundred days, the *Resolution* dropped anchor at Easter Island.
Here William Hodges painted a striking view of several gigantic grey and red statues rising skyward against dark green

storm clouds. Anders Sparrman observed that the cylindrical red headpieces of these giants were "so accurately proportioned that they might have been turned with lathes." Sparrman looked about in vain for the source of the yellowish grey sandstone which composed the statues. Had he found his way across the island to a volcanic crater name Rano Raraku, he might have come upon dozens of these tight-lipped, long-eared giants lying among the rocks from which they were hewn.[15] The island itself, lacking trees and scattered over with stones, seemed uninviting to the voyagers, and food and water were scarce.

Passing through the southern Marquesas, the *Resolution* spent four days at the island of Tahu Ata, in the identical bay where Mendaña, the Spanish discoverer of the islands, had anchored in 1595. No European had visited the Marquesas since that time, and their location on the charts had been uncertain.[16]

Several atolls were sighted and named as the *Resolution* made for Tahiti, and on April 22nd, after an absence of nearly eight months, Cook reached his former base at Point Venus. His first object in touching again at Tahiti was to give William Wales an opportunity to check the experimental timepieces against a known longitude. Opportunity was also taken to repair the ship's rigging and ironwork and to air and sort the stale bread. The botanists made two overnight excursions toward

15. See Thor Heyerdahl, *Aku-Aku, The Secret of Easter Island* (Chicago, 1958), pp. 85ff.

16. Cook did not touch at the island of Hiva-Oa, where Paul Gauguin now lies buried, although he sailed along its coast, nor did he see Nuku-Hiva in the northern Marquesas, where Herman Melville jumped ship in 1842.

the summit of a nearby mountain, a position from which they could see the neighboring island of Huahine and look down upon the valleys far below. "In the roadstead we saw the *Resolution*, a dot in the blue immensity, and it astonished us to think that we had voyaged so far on board that little vessel." George Forster made a special study of the edible plants of the island, a subject he later used as the basis for his doctoral dissertation. He also found time to make sketches of a dozen or so Tahitian birds. Among his drawings of parrots, pigeons, warblers, and swallows is a sketch of the now-extinct white-winged sandpiper and a painting of the bristle-thighed curlew, a bird whose summer nesting place near the Yukon River in Alaska was not discovered until 1948.[17]

A spectacular fleet of native war canoes, preparing to sail against the island of Moorea, had not yet departed when the *Resolution* left Tahiti on May 14th. Running for a second time through the Tonga archipelago, north of Tongatapu, the ship stopped briefly at Nomuka and then continued northwestward toward an area where two earlier explorers had reported land. In 1606 the Spanish visionary Quiros had believed that his "Austrialia del Espiritu Santo" was a part of the fabled southern continent; and in 1768, sailing in the same vicinity, the French explorer Bougainville had passed through a cluster

17. See Arthur A. Allen, "The Curlew's Secret," *The National Geographic Magazine*, Vol. 94, No. 6 (December 1948), pp. 751-770. George Forster's painting of the bristle-thighed curlew is reproduced in *The Illustrated London News* (June 26, 1948), p. 724. An annotated catalog of bird drawings by George Forster will be found in Averil Lysaght, "Some Eighteenth Century Bird Paintings in the Library of Sir Joseph Banks," *British Museum [Natural History] Bulletin, Historical Series*, Vol. 1, No. 6 (April 1959), pp. 280-310.

of islands which are shown on his chart as the "Great Cyclades." After weathering a gale which split several sails, Cook in mid-July sighted Bougainville's Aurora Island (now known as Maewo) and thereupon spent six weeks surveying the long chain of islands which he renamed the New Hebrides.

His first anchorage was at Malekula Island, where the chestnut-brown natives, wearing nose-sticks and hog-tusk bracelets, were obviously a different race from the Polynesians. If to European eyes they seemed less attractive than the Tahitians or the beautiful Marquesans, they were quick and intelligent. George Forster remarked their facility in imitating sounds; they could easily pronounce most European words, he said, even the Russian "shch." [18] Only one small pig and a few cocoanuts could be obtained as provisions, and so Cook remained at Malekula but thirty-six hours, long enough to make a chart of the harbor. At Eromanga, nearly 200 miles to the southeast, Cook landed in Polenia Bay and went ashore toward a throng of armed natives with a green branch of peace in his hand. Apparently he was mistaken for a ghost. When the crowd tried to haul his boat up the beach, he was forced to retreat amid salvos of arrows, stones, and darts. His pique at this turn of events is apparent on modern maps of Eromanga, where the headland south of his anchorage is still known as Traitor's Head.

His lengthiest stay in the New Hebrides was at the island of Tana. Again the natives were threatening, but the noise of

18. For a vividly factual account of the inhabitants of this "least-known" island in the New Hebrides, see T. H. Harrisson, "Living with the People of Malekula," *The Geographical Journal*, Vol. 88, No. 2 (August 1936), pp. 97-127.

cannon fire from the ship cleared a beach which Cook roped off for his waterers and woodcutters. Day by day the natives became less menacing, and gradually the botanists were able to extend their excursions beyond the beach and into the magnificent forests, where orchids and yellow crotons flowered among the banyan trees. A few miles from the anchorage an active volcano rumbled intermittently and spewed up clouds of eye-stinging ashes. Though Cook and his companions remained on the island less than three weeks, their observations have ethnographic value as records of the first contact between Europeans and the Melanesian inhabitants of Tana.

From Tana, Cook sailed north along the western side of the long chain of islands, past Efate and into the Bougainville Strait, which forms a passage between Malekula and a large island to the north. He completed his survey of the archipelago by circling around this island, where he identified the deep bay at the north as Quiros' Bay of St. Philip and St. James. On Cook's chart, Quiros' continent was resolved into Espiritu Santo, the northernmost island of the New Hebrides.

Four days after leaving the New Hebrides, Cook discovered New Caledonia. His reason for assigning this name to the island is uncertain. Possibly the blue and misty purple of its rugged mountains reminded someone on the *Resolution* of the highlands of Scotland. The ship anchored near a small sandy island from which Cook and Wales and Lieutenant Clerke observed an eclipse of the sun and determined the longitude. Fresh water was available but provisions were scarce. The natives, Cook wrote, "had little else but good nature to spare us." From the hills Cook and an excursion party saw the western

39

coast of the island and observed a system of canals by which the natives irrigated their taro plantations.

Unable to get through the reefs at the north of New Caledonia, Cook sailed nearly 250 miles to the southeastern coast. He found dangerous reefs surrounding nearly the entire island. At the southern end and on adjacent small islands, strange clusters of towering pillars were sighted. Cook and his officers believed these to be trees of an unusual kind, but the elder Forster declared them to be pillars of basalt and averred that he could see their joints very distinctly through his spyglass. At considerable risk Cook maneuvered through the reefs to one of the islands and determined that the pillars were indeed a kind of spruce pine, now known as pencil pines or Cook pines, which grow 100 feet tall or higher. Against the sky, says one observer, they look like giant asphodels.[19]

The approach of the austral summer and the difficulty of carrying on a coastal survey among dangerous reefs impelled Cook to leave New Caledonia at the end of September. Ten days later, some 400 miles from New Zealand, he discovered an uninhabited island where flax, cabbage palms, and tall pine trees were growing luxuriantly. This was Norfolk Island, which in the mid-nineteenth century was to become notorious as a penal colony for twice-condemned convicts.[20] Incongruous it may seem, but in the 1880's, for a chapel built on this

19. Roderick Cameron, *The Golden Haze: With Captain Cook in the South Pacific* (Cleveland, 1964), p. 240.

20. The island figures in Marcus Clarke's *For the Term of His Natural Life* (1874), a novel which strongly indicted the British convict-transportation system. There is a recent popularized account of the curious history of this island: Frank Clune, *The Norfolk Island Story* (Sydney, 1967).

remote island, Burne-Jones designed stained-glass windows which were executed by William Morris.

After a third period of recuperation at Queen Charlotte's Sound in New Zealand, where the ship was recaulked, the rigging overhauled, and supplies of fish and fresh water laid in, the *Resolution* made a rapid run of forty-two days to the southern tip of South America. Sighting Cape Deseado at the western outlet of the Straits of Magellan, Cook began charting the broken coastline of Tierra del Fuego. A few days before Christmas he anchored in a sheltered bay where an abundance of wild geese, shell fish, and terns' eggs together with the remaining Madeira wine ("the only one of our provisions that had improved during the long voyage") provided a satisfactory Christmas dinner. The botanists gathered a variety of plants, including the aromatic Winter's bark, and William Hodges painted an impressive view of Christmas Sound which was later engraved for Cook's official account. George Forster took exception to Hodges' representation in this painting of a hawk "which, from its supernatural size, seems to resemble the rukh, celebrated in the Arabian Tales."

On December 28th the *Resolution* rounded the black cliffs of Cape Horn in good weather and spent the first days of January, 1775, at Staten Island, where hundreds of seals and penguins were seen. Sailing into the South Atlantic Ocean, Cook searched fruitlessly for the "Gulf of San Sebastian" which Dalrymple's charts alleged to be a part of the fabled southern continent. He then bore up to the northeast, looking for land which had been sighted through the fogs in 1675 by Antonio de la Roche. On January 14th he saw what at first appeared to

be an immense iceberg; it proved to be a rocky and moun-
tainous land almost wholly covered with snow. Through
storms of snow and sleet Cook began charting the northern
coast, and on the 17th he and the botanists landed in a small
boat. Tussock grass and wild burnet grew sparsely on the
coast, and in the bays ice was seen breaking from the glacier
walls. Seals swarmed on the shores and flocks of penguins three
feet tall resembled those described by Bougainville, with
"belly of a dazzling white and a kind of palatine or necklace of
bright yellow." Thinking that at last he might have reached
the southern continent, Cook continued his survey, only to
find that he was circling round an island. It is known today as
the island of South Georgia.

Moving southeastward through thick fogs, the *Resolution*
pushed toward the 60th parallel. Numerous whales were seen.
Once again land was sighted, snow-covered peaks with inter-
vening pack ice which made it impossible for Cook to determine whether these peaks formed one connected land or
several distinct islands. On his map he laid down several capes
and a few islands and, perhaps with a touch of weariness after
so long a voyage, decided that this snow-burdened land was so
forbidding that it did not warrant the risk of further exploration. "The risk one runs in exploring a coast in these unknown
and icy seas is so very great," Cook wrote, "that I can be bold
to say that no man will ever venture farther than I have done
and that the lands which may lie to the south will never be
explored."

Cook underestimated the equipment and perseverance of his
successors. Some forty years later Bellingshausen determined

that the peaks Cook had seen were indeed islands (the South Sandwich Islands), in the nineteenth century Wilkes and Ross roughly surveyed Antarctica, and in the twentieth century the continent was to be explored by Scott, Shackleton, Amundsen, and Byrd. Cook's own report of whales and seals in the South Atlantic rapidly led to commercial exploitation of the area, and by the 1820's more than a million fur seals had been taken in South Georgia. Cook's demonstration was that the southern continent does not extend above the 60th parallel. Although he did not set foot on the polar continent itself, the history of Antarctica begins with his circumnavigation on this second voyage.[21]

Cook's official account of the voyage, illustrated with more than sixty engravings based on views and portraits drawn by William Hodges, was published in 1777.[22] By that time Cook had long since departed on his third voyage, and the volumes were seen through the press by Canon John Douglas, the man who had earlier vindicated John Milton from charges of plagiarism and with Samuel Johnson had exposed the fraudulence of the Cock Lane ghost. The two handsome volumes of the original edition are classic and have not been completely

21. No fewer than 640 antarctic expeditions are known to have taken place between Cook's second voyage and the beginning of the International Geophysical Year in July, 1957. See Brian Roberts, "Chronological List of Antarctic Expeditions," *The Polar Record*, Vol. 9, No. 59 (May 1958), pp. 97-134 and No. 60 (September 1958), pp. 191-239.
22. James Cook, *A Voyage towards the South Pole, and Round the World. Performed in His Majesty's Ships the Resolution and Adventure, in the Years 1772, 1773, 1774, and 1775. . . . In which is included Captain Furneaux's Narrative of his Proceedings in the Adventure during the Separation of the Ships. . . .* 2 vols. (London, 1777). A facsimile edition was published in Adelaide in 1970 by the Library Board of South Australia (Australiana Facsimile Editions no. 191).

superseded even by the masterful modern edition of J. C. Beaglehole.[23] Beaglehole's minutely-annotated edition is based upon Cook's two holograph journals in the British Museum supplemented by three early manuscript copies. His edition also prints, with some excisions, the journal of William Wales from an incomplete manuscript in the Mitchell Library, Sydney, together with extracts from the manuscript logs kept by several of the ships' officers.

For reasons which have yet to be satisfactorily elucidated, J. R. Forster after his return was forbidden by Lord Sandwich to write any "connected narrative" of the voyage.[24] His son George thereupon set about writing a detailed account which reached publication a few weeks before Cook's official volumes.[25] Despite the rapidity of its composition, it is a surprisingly good book. It has its purple passages and its petulance, and Samuel Johnson was exaggerating no more than usual when he remarked that "there is a great affectation of fine writing in it," but it deserves to be better known. In Germany it was influential, Gottfried Bürger, for example, drawing

23. J. C. Beaglehole, ed., *The Journals of Captain James Cook on His Voyages of Discovery, Vol. 2: The Voyage of the* Resolution *and* Adventure, *1772-1775* (Cambridge, 1959).

24. In an open letter published as a pamphlet, George Forster traced his father's difficulties to Martha Ray, mistress of Lord Sandwich, who was allegedly angered at J. R. Forster's refusal to give to her a collection of live birds he had intended as a gift for the Queen. See George Forster, *A Letter to the Right Honourable The Earl of Sandwich, First Lord Commissioner of the Board of Admiralty. . . .* (London, 1778). This pamphlet has been called "one of the most forcibly virulent attacks on a prominent politician known to English literature."

25. George Forster, *A Voyage Round the World in His Britannic Majesty's Sloop, Resolution, commanded by Capt. James Cook, during the Years 1772, 3, 4, and 5.* 2 vols. (London, 1777).

from it parts of his poem *Neuseeländisches Schlachtlied.*[26] In England it was attacked by the usually calm William Wales.[27] There is need for a modern edition of George Forster's *A Voyage Round the World* which would draw annotations from Wales, provide a generous selection from George's many unpublished drawings, and shed light on the relationship of the book to J. R. Forster's still-unpublished journals.[28] Happily a German edition of George Forster's collected works, currently in progress, has reprinted the original English text of the book as well as the German translation.[29] In this edition, George's account of the voyage is characterized as "one of the greatest travelogues written in any tongue or age."

The third principal narrative account of the voyage, in addition to the volumes by Cook and by Forster, is that of Anders Sparrman, the assistant naturalist. His account was originally published in Swedish in two parts, the first of which appeared in 1802 and the second not until 1818.[30] A partial

26. J. A. Asher, "Georg Forster and Goethe," *AUMLA, Journal of the Australasian Universities Language and Literature Association,* No. 7 (November 1957), pp. 16-17.

27. William Wales, *Remarks on Mr. Forster's Account of Captain Cook's last Voyage round the World, In the Years 1772, 1773, 1774, and 1775* (London, 1778). George Forster replied to this attack in his pamphlet *Reply to Mr. Wales's Remarks* (London, 1778).

28. According to Robert L. Kahn, J. R. Forster's six-volume manuscript journal is MSS Germ. quart. 222-227 of the Deutsche Staatsbibliothek, Berlin, currently Staatsbibliothek der Stiftung Preussischer Kulturbesitz, West Berlin.

29. *Georg Forsters Werke: Sämtliche Schriften, Tagebücher, Briefe,* Bd. 1: *A Voyage Round the World,* bearb. von Robert L. Kahn (Berlin, 1968).

30. An earlier volume by Sparrman appeared in Sweden in 1783 and was translated into English in 1785 under the title *A Voyage to the Cape of Good Hope.* . . . It deals principally with South Africa and is not to be confused with his later related volumes.

translation into French became available in 1939.[31] There was no English translation of these volumes until 1944, when the Golden Cockerel Press issued a beautifully-produced limited edition of 350 copies.[32] This is a worthy supplement to the earlier accounts by Sparrman's colleagues. Its brevity and sprightliness recommend it as perhaps the easiest introduction to the full story of Captain Cook's second voyage—possibly the greatest voyage between the time of Magellan and the flight of Apollo Eleven.

31. [Anders Sparrman] *Un Compagnon Suédois du Capitaine James Cook au Cours de Son Deuxième Voyage*, tr. Bjarne Kroepelien (Oslo, 1939).

32. Anders Sparrman, *A Voyage Round the World with Captain James Cook in H.M.S. Resolution* (London, 1944). A trade edition was published in London by Robert Hale in 1953.

III

The Third Voyage
1776-1780

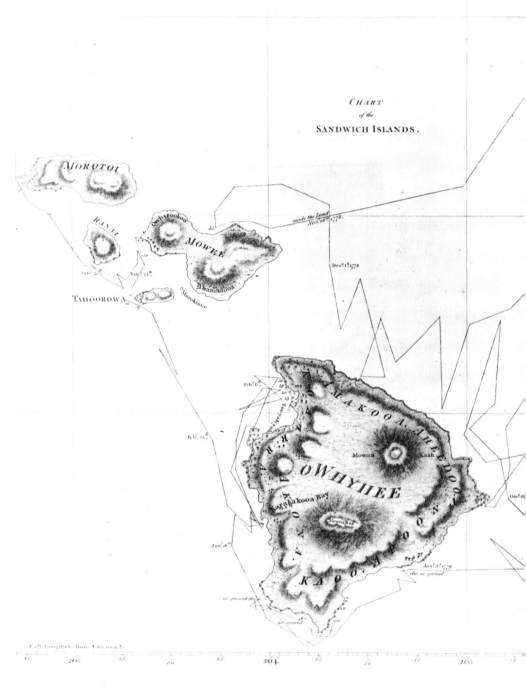

On September 20, 1969, when the 150,000-ton tanker *Manhattan* (Captain Roger Steward) reached Point Barrow, Alaska, having left the shipyards at Chester, Pennsylvania, less than a month earlier, she became the first commercial ship to sail the Northwest Passage. It was not the silks and spices of Cathay but the effort to transport oil from Prudhoe Bay on Alaska's northern slope that gave incentive for this historic voyage.

In the years following the first transit of the Northwest Passage, completed between 1903 and 1906 by Roald Amundsen in a 47-ton herring boat, the route had been sailed by Canadian and United States government ships and by the nuclear submarines *Nautilus*, *Skate*, and *Seadragon*. But the centuries-old hope for a northern passage that would be commercially useful was not realized until the successful round-trip voyage of the gigantic *Manhattan* in 1969.

Most of the early efforts to find a Northwest Passage had been directed at the eastern side of the American continent, and such geographical features as Frobisher Bay, Davis Strait, Hudson Bay, and Baffin Island memorialize the names of certain of the sixteenth and seventeenth century seekers of the passage. The western side of the North American continent was probed in 1579 by Sir Francis Drake, who sailed northward in the *Golden Hinde*, past San Francisco Bay, and along the coast of "New Albion" as far north, it has been claimed, as Vancouver Island. After Drake, the north Pacific remained so little known that in the seventeenth century Francis Bacon could situate his Utopian New Atlantis in this "greatest Wildernesse of Waters in the World," and Jonathan Swift in the eighteenth century could place Gulliver's giants of Brobdingnag on a peninsula jutting westward into the Bering Sea.

In 1776 the British Admiralty renewed the search for a Northwest Passage and instructed Captain Cook to proceed to the "Coast of New Albion" to look for a waterway leading from the Pacific Ocean into the Atlantic Ocean or the North Sea. Cook, in fact, volunteered for this duty, but he was a tired man, and there were to be times during the ensuing voyage when his nerves seemed as frayed as the tattered rigging on his ships.

THE THIRD VOYAGE
1776-1780

⚓

In the wartime shipyards at Deptford the *Resolution* (Captain Cook) and her consort ship the *Discovery* (Captain Charles Clerke) were fitted out rather poorly, as time was to show, and Cook sailed from Plymouth Sound on July 12, 1776, leaving the *Discovery* to follow as soon as her captain could extricate himself from debtor's prison. Impatient at the slowness of the law courts, Captain Clerke decamped from the Fleet prison late in July and went immediately to Cawsand Bay, where James Burney, his first lieutenant, had the ship in readiness, and on August 1st the *Discovery* sailed on a nonstop passage to Capetown.

From Capetown, where the *Discovery* arrived early in November, three weeks after the *Resolution* had anchored, Cook sent a friendly letter to William Hodges, who had been official artist on his second voyage, and to William Strahan his publisher; and James King, astronomer and second lieutenant of the *Resolution*, wrote to his friends Jane and Edmund Burke.[1] The surgeon of the *Resolution*, William Anderson, found time to make a wagon trip to Stellenbosch, where he examined

---

1. One of Lieutenant James King's younger brothers, the Reverend Dr. Walker King, was later to serve as a literary executor for Edmund Burke, in which capacity he helped to edit the collection of Burke's *Works* that appeared between 1792 and 1827.

a granite boulder of "prodigious size" and sent a description of it to the Royal Society. In the absence of an official scientist for the expedition, Anderson was to give some attention to natural history, and the *Discovery* carried a gardener from Kew, David Nelson, who was collecting for Joseph Banks.[2]

In conformity with his instructions from the Admiralty, Cook sailed from Capetown into the Indian Ocean to determine the location of an island lately discovered by the French. This was Kerguelen Island, which the ships sighted through the fogs in late December. Cook sent his young sailing-master, William Bligh, to look for a harbor, and on December 25th the ships dropped anchor in Christmas Harbor, where the shores were lined with rows of tall penguins looking like a regiment of soldiers. Grass was cut for the livestock and supplies of water and seal blubber were taken in. Among the boggy declivities Anderson and Nelson collected specimens of an edible plant which the whalers of the next century were to call Macquarie's cabbage, and one of the sailors found a bottle with a note inside which had apparently been left by Kerguelen's consort ship *Oiseau*. Cook added a few lines to this note, dropped in a silver tuppence, and replaced the bottle, which was reportedly carried off sixteen years later by the American brig *Ino*.

At the end of December the ships sailed eastward, through thick patches of kelp or seaweed that lie off Kerguelen Island,

---

2. David Nelson is the subject of a brief chapter in a delightful little book by A. W. Anderson, *How We Got Our Flowers* (London, 1956), pp. 143-149. Nelson was among those set adrift by the mutineers on the *Bounty*, but after enduring the rigors of that famous 3,600 mile open-boat voyage to Timor with Captain Bligh, he died at Coupang in 1789.

and less than a month later they touched at Adventure Bay in Tasmania, where on Cook's second voyage the *Adventure* (Captain Furneaux) had paused. The natives were unarmed and quite naked, and James Burney noted in his journal that they "have much less idea of decency than an English dog." Among the plants that David Nelson collected in Tasmania was an acacia with lemon-yellow blossoms which is still sometimes known as Nelson's mimosa.

Nearly two weeks in February were spent at Queen Charlotte's Sound in New Zealand, where wood and water were plentiful. Copper boilers were set up on shore to melt down the seal blubber obtained at Kerguelen Island, and though this processing was intended to produce lamp oil, one of the assistant surgeons, David Samwell, noted that the New Zealanders were extremely fond of this "delicate food." Cook and Clerke with an armed party visited Grass Cove, where Furneaux's boat crew had been massacred on the previous voyage, and found out some details regarding that affair. Cook saw little point in avenging the massacre, though the natives were contemptuous of his restraint, and John Webber, the official artist of the expedition, was so bold as to sketch a portrait of Kahura, the chief instigator of the massacre. What astonished the New Zealanders most was the sight of the horses, cattle, sheep, and goats that Cook was transporting to Tahiti.

Light and insufficient winds delayed the expedition northeast of New Zealand, and it became apparent that the work of exploring the northwest coast of America would have to wait till the following summer. After sighting three new islands in the southern Cook group, on one of which a small landing-party was detained for a day by inscrutable natives, the ships touched briefly at Palmerston Island. Here cocoanuts were gathered, grass was cut for the livestock, and Surgeon Anderson was enchanted by the branching coral in one of the lagoons where colorful fish swam placidly in the bright water.

The ships tarried for nearly ten weeks among the islands of the Tonga archipelago, and William Bligh was able to make a detailed chart of the group. David Samwell found Nomuka to be "as beautiful a spot as imagination can paint," and he amused himself shooting wild ducks at a large lagoon while shore parties under Lieutenant King's direction were buying hogs and other provisions and carrying on a surreptitious trade for red feathers. At Lifuka in mid-May the voyagers were entertained with wrestling and boxing matches and wild native dances, to which they reciprocated by putting their marines through maneuvers ("a most ludicrous performance," said William Bligh) and shooting off an impressive display of fireworks. Cook and his men were unaware that the chiefs of these Friendly Islands had planned this night's entertainment as an ambush, which failed to kindle only because the chiefs could not agree among themselves on the best time to strike.[3]

As the ships approached Tahiti in August, Omai, the "noble savage" who had fluttered the fashionable circles of London two years earlier, "sat all day on the forecastle viewing his native shores with tears in his eyes." Tents and observatories were again erected at Point Venus, and the mainmast of the

3. Information concerning this planned assault on Cook and his men was obtained by William Mariner, who was a captive in the Tonga Islands from 1805 to 1810. See John Martin, *An Account of the Natives of the Tonga Islands* (Boston, 1820), pp. 304-305.

Discovery was hauled on shore for repairs. Shortly before his departure, Captain Cook observed a sacrificial ceremony, the human victim having been killed the night before. In John Webber's watercolor drawing of this ritual event, the skulls of some fifty former victims can be seen in the background, and this macabre picture, which was engraved for the official account of the voyage, became one of the best-known illustrations of the century.

Pilfering by the natives was a constant annoyance. At Tonga several indispensable cats had been spirited from the rat-infested ships, and while on shore duty Lieutenant Molesworth Phillips of the marines had had his bed stolen, "some say from under him while he was asleep." At Moorea Cook was so incensed by the disappearance of two goats that he set fire to a village and destroyed a number of canoes, and at Huahine a "hardened scoundrel" who stole a brass sextant was punished by having both his ears cut off. Not all of Cook's officers condoned this severity, and Captain Clerke usually punished such offenders by shaving half of the thief's head, one eyebrow, and half his beard, "which effectually rid us of his company till his hair grew again."

Omai having decided to settle at Huahine, the carpenters of both ships built a small house for him where he could lock up the treasures he had brought back with him from England— a barrel-organ, a jack-in-the-box, some toy soldiers, sky rockets, a musket, a bayonet, two pairs of pistols with swords, cutlasses, and ammunition. When William Bligh returned to Tahiti in 1788 on his ill-fated breadfruit voyage, he learned that Omai had died of natural causes some thirty months after Cook had left him.[4]

During the month the ships lay at Raiatea, one of the marines from the *Resolution* abandoned his sentry post and disappeared into the night. After he was found and brought back, a midshipman and the gunner's mate from the *Discovery* both deserted. Determined to recover these men, Cook detained the son, daughter, and son-in-law of the island chieftain on board his ship and held them as hostages until the natives located the English fugitives at Bora-Bora and brought them back. It was at this time, while she was a prisoner on the *Resolution*, that John Webber painted a portrait of Poetua, the chieftain's daughter.

> John Webber's *Poedooa* is a highly romantic image of a firm-breasted young Raiatean girl bare to the waist, who wears the flowers of the cape jasmine in her hair and a Gioconda look upon her face. She represents both the mysteries of the East and the sensual pleasures of Tahiti, the sailor's paradise.[5]

After crossing the equator in late December, the ships came upon a low crescent-shaped atoll, Christmas Island, where vast numbers of green turtles were procured, though two seamen

4. The account of Omai's return in the official narrative of Cook's third voyage revived public interest in Omai. William Cowper, in the first book of his poem *The Task* (1785), waxed indignant over the fate of this gentle savage, and a stage production by John O'Keefe, *Omai: or a Trip Round the World*, with costumes and scenery by de Loutherbourg, was a smashing success at the Theatre Royal during the Christmas season of 1785. See William Huse, "A Noble Savage on the Stage," *Modern Philology*, Vol. 33, No. 3 (February 1936), pp. 303-316.

5. This is Bernard Smith's description of Webber's painting in *European Vision and the South Pacific, 1768-1850* (Oxford, 1960), p. 93.

got lost on the little island and nearly perished from heat and thirst.

At dawn on the morning of January 18, 1778, the *Resolution* and the *Discovery* saw high land to windward. This was the beginning of the recorded history of Hawaii. Oahu was sighted first, but the winds favored an approach to Kauai, and a landing in small boats was made at Waimea Bay, where a native was killed in a scuffle over a boat-hook. At Niihau a few days later, Lieutenant Gore and a party went ashore to trade for salt and yams and were stranded on the beach for two nights before the boats could take them off through the high surf. Cook fixed the position of these westward islands of the Hawaiian group, and he suspected that others would be found to the east, but a fuller survey was deferred as the ships pressed northward to look for a northwest passage.

While still some days from the American coast, Surgeon Anderson observed a strange phosphorescence in the waters around the *Resolution*. Taking up a sample of seawater, he described the tiny sea-medusae in a page that was later to stir the imagination of Coleridge the poet:

> They [the small sea animals] emitted the brightest colours of the most precious gems ... assuming various tints of blue, from a pale sapphirine to a deep violet colour ... frequently mixed with a ruby, or opaline redness. ... With candle light, the colour was, chiefly, a beautiful, pale green, tinged with a burnished gloss; and, in the dark, it had a faint appearance of glowing fire.[6]

6. "Few passages, indeed, which Coleridge ever read seem to have fecundated his imagination so amazingly as that 257th page of Cook's second volume, which described the 'small sea animals swimming about' in 'a kind of slime' with 'a faint appearance of glowing fire.'" John Livingston Lowes, *The Road to Xanadu* (Boston, 1927), p. 90.

The coast of present-day Oregon was sighted on March 7, but storms off Cape Foulweather drove the ships southward, and it was not until two weeks later that an indentation in the coastline to the north gave promise of a harbor. Disappointingly, low land seemed to close this opening, and Cook named the point Cape Flattery. He did not realize that his ships were within a few miles of the entrance to the Strait of Juan de Fuca leading to the lovely inland waters of Puget Sound.

About one hundred miles northwest of Cape Flattery the ships found anchorage in Nootka Sound, at a spot still known as Resolution Cove on Bligh Island. Here the foremast of the *Resolution* was unstepped and taken on shore for repair, sails and rigging were mended, supplies of wood and water replenished, and a quantity of spruce beer was brewed. The natives eagerly traded fine sea-otter furs and bearskins for brass buttons, pewter plates, and broken pans and kettles. Sometimes at dusk they appeared in masks of cedarwood carved to resemble the heads of deer or birds and paddled round the ships singing wild songs, to which the Englishmen responded with French horns and a fife and drum. Cook, Clerke, and some others visited a native village at nearby Yuquot Point, where John Webber made drawings of rude dwellings, totems, and primitive implements.[7] During the next quarter-century Nootka Sound was to become one of the most-frequented harbors on the northwest coast of America, but Cook did not stay long enough to discover the precise geographical nature of this re-

7. Some of these were engraved for the official account, but see also David I. Bushnell, Jr., "Drawings by John Webber of Natives of the Northwest Coast of America, 1778," *Smithsonian Miscellaneous Collections*, Vol. 80, No. 10 (March 24, 1928), pp. 1-16.

gion. It remained for George Vancouver, one of the midshipmen on the *Discovery*, to return in 1792 to circumnavigate Vancouver Island and survey in detail the coastline from California to Alaska.[8]

Leaving Nootka Sound in late April, the ships bore away to the northwest, and on May 4th they sighted a volcanic mountain which they identified as Mount St. Elias, the landmark that had been Vitus Bering's first sight of the American coast in 1741. Cook and Anderson landed briefly on Kayak Island, where Steller, the naturalist with Bering, had collected for ten hours,[9] and a few days later the ships dropped anchor in Prince William Sound to repair a leak in the *Resolution*. Natives came off in kayaks, and noting that the hats of these Eskimos were ornamented with glass beads, Cook surmised that Russians from Kamchatka had been trading for furs along this coast.

Two weeks in early June were consumed in exploring that vast arm of the sea which is known today as Cook Inlet. William Bligh looked into the Knik estuary and landed on Fire Island near the site of present-day Anchorage, and Lieutenant King hoisted the English colors at Possession Point. Through mist and fogs the ships traced the coast past Kodiak Island, the Shumagins, and Unimak Island in the Aleutians. By the

8. Vancouver's classic account, with an accompanying atlas of maps and plates, was published in 1798 as *A Voyage of Discovery to the North Pacific Ocean, and Round the World; In Which the Coast of North-West America Has Been Carefully Examined and Accurately Surveyed.* 4 vols. A facsimile reprint of this first edition was published in 1968.

9. For an excellent account of Vitus Bering's second voyage, with a focus on the naturalist George Wilhelm Steller, see Corey Ford, *Where the Sea Breaks Its Back* (Boston, 1966).

end of June the ships were anchored in Samganuda Harbor on Unalaska Island. It was clear that the Russians were well known at Samganuda (now called English Bay), for the natives bowed and doffed their hats as they came alongside, and they were eager to trade for tobacco and snuff. Captain Cook and a party entertained themselves by shooting grouse, while David Samwell, John Webber, and some others visited a native village. The houses resembled small hillocks of earth, and Samwell noted that "the whole town stinks worse than a tanner's yard." Webber made sketches of the houses and of a "very beautiful" young woman, and David Nelson collected specimens of an Aleutian buttercup which still bears his name (*Ranunculus Nelsoni*).

From Samganuda Harbor the ships emerged in the Bering Sea and spent the first two weeks of July tracing the shores of Bristol Bay. A boat was sent ashore briefly at Cape Newenham, where deer and foxes were seen, and at the end of the month Cook sighted St. Matthew Island and remarked on the myriads of sea birds flying round its perpendicular cliffs. Surgeon Anderson, ill from tuberculosis, died on August 3rd and was buried at sea a day or two before the ships sighted St. Lawrence Island.[10] On August 9th, sailing through Bering Strait, Cook named the western extremity of America after the Prince of Wales and passed the twin Diomede Islands, which lie midway between Cape Prince of Wales and the Siberian mainland.

10. A survey of Anderson's career is attempted by J. J. Keevil, "William Anderson, 1748-1778, Master Surgeon, Royal Navy," *Annals of Medical History,* new series, Vol. 5, No. 6 (November 1933), pp. 511-524.

Before the ships sailed northward into the Arctic Ocean, Cook landed for two or three hours at a village on the Asian shore, and John Webber drew sketches of the Chukchi natives. During the next week the two ships pushed as far north as 70° 44′, just beyond Icy Cape, where further progress was blocked by unexpected pack ice. At this point Cook was almost as close to the North Pole as he had been to the South Pole on his previous voyage. It was probably fortunate that he had not arrived a few weeks earlier, when the pack ice usually retreats briefly from the Alaskan shore, for if he had tried to push past Point Barrow it is likely that his ships would have been locked in the ice forever.

From Icy Cape the ships sailed south and then westward for a week, along a wall of ice sometimes ten or twelve feet high. Occasionally the fogs lifted to reveal herds of walrus on the ice.[11] Moving down the Siberian coast past Serdtse-Kamen, Cook again reached Bering Strait, accurately determined the position of the easternmost tip of Asia, and resolved to return the following summer to make another northern exploration.

To assure himself that Alaska was not an island, as it was represented on Stählin's map of 1774, Cook crossed again to the American coast looking for a possible channel. In early September the ships anchored for a week in Norton Sound, which Cook named after Lieutenant King's relative, Sir Fletcher Norton, then Speaker of the House of Commons. Lieutenant King took two small boats northward to explore

11. At first these animals were thought to be sea cows of the kind Steller had described, but that curious creature was extinct even in Cook's time and is known today only by a bone or two in the Leningrad Academy of Sciences.

the inlet, the men relaxed ashore and picked wild raspberries and currants, while Cook made seventy-seven sets of lunar observations to check his longitude.

A few days after the vessels had anchored for a second time in Samganuda Harbor, a native accompanied by two Asiatics came to Cook bringing a present of spiced salmon baked in a rye loaf, and from this gift Cook inferred that there were Russians somewhere on the island. Corporal John Ledyard of the marines, a native of Connecticut, volunteered to return with these messengers and make contact with the Russians.[12] On Cook's advice Ledyard went unarmed, taking only some bread and brandy and a few bottles of rum and wine as a gift. After a circuitous day-and-a-half journey by foot and by water, Ledyard arrived at a village somewhere on Iliuliuk Bay, probably near the site of the present U. S. Naval base at Dutch Harbor, where he found some thirty Russians and twice that many Asiatics from Kamchatka. Three of these Russian fur hunters returned with Ledyard, and in a few days Gerasim Izmailov, the captain of the Russian sloop *St. Paul*, which Ledyard had seen anchored at Dutch Harbor, came to see

12. There is room for a scholarly biography of John Ledyard, who was later to have interesting contacts with Robert Morris, Thomas Jefferson, John Paul Jones, Lafayette, and Joseph Banks. Two twentieth-century biographies have so far appeared, but both are popular rather than scholarly: Kenneth Munford, *John Ledyard: An American Marco Polo* (Portland, Oregon, 1939) and Helen Augur, *Passage to Glory: John Ledyard's America* (Garden City, N.Y., 1946). The best life of Ledyard is still the outdated nineteenth-century study by Jared Sparks, *The Life of John Ledyard, the American Traveller*, 2d. ed. (Cambridge, Mass., 1829). Material relating to Ledyard's unsuccessful attempt to cross Russia and Siberia will be found in Stephen D. Watrous, ed., *John Ledyard's Journey through Russia and Siberia, 1787-1788: The Journal and Selected Letters* (Madison, 1966).

Cook, and the two captains compared charts and exchanged information, though they had to converse by signs and figures. Against the expedition's planned return the next summer, Izmailov gave Cook letters of introduction to the Governor of Kamchatka and to the commanding officer at Petropavlovsk, and Cook entrusted Izmailov with a letter to the British Admiralty, enclosing a chart of his discoveries, which Izmailov promised to forward via Siberia and St. Petersburg.[13]

In late October the ships left the Aleutians and sailed for the Hawaiian Islands. One month later they sighted the island of Maui and lay off shore trading with natives who came alongside in canoes. For seven weeks the ships cruised around Hawaii searching for a harbor, while the sailors grew increasingly restive. Trying to get round Cape Kumuhaki, the eastern tip of Hawaii, the ships lost sight of each other during a heavy rainstorm and parted company for nearly two weeks. It was not until mid-January that William Bligh found a bay on the western side of Hawaii, Kealakekua Bay, where the ships could anchor.

When Captain Cook went ashore, the natives fell on their hands and knees, and he was led to a place sacred to Lono, a deity of Hawaiian mythology. Here, with songs or incantations and surrounded by strange images and human skulls, Cook was wrapped in a red cloth and fed some barbecued pig. Whether or not the natives considered him to be an incarnation of Lono is a moot point. In later ceremonies, an offering

13. This letter and map eventually reached London on March 6, 1780. The map is reproduced as Chart XLIX in the portfolio accompanying Beaglehole's edition of Cook, and the text of the letter is given in Beaglehole's volume 3, part 2, pp. 1530-1533.

was burnt before him, and Cook placed a gift of beads beside one of the images.

The observatories were erected in a sweet-potato field near the sacred enclosure, and the natives apparently concluded that the astronomers' clocks and watches were the gods which the Englishmen worshipped. In a few days King Kalaniopuu with some of his chiefs, dressed in cloaks of brilliant red and yellow feathers, visited Cook and with great ceremony made him a present of seven or eight magnificent feathered capes. When David Nelson, George Vancouver, John Ledyard and some others set out to climb the heights toward Mauna Loa, they noticed, among the dense forest growth that blocked their way, many of the bright birds whose plumage was used in these feathered cloaks. The tops of the lofty ohia trees were frequented by a black bird, the o-o, whose wing tufts were of a fine crocus yellow, and among the tree-ferns and lobelias darted the scarlet iiwi, whose breast feathers were used in the Hawaiian capes and leis. Specimens of these and other birds were collected, and drawings of them were made by John Webber and by William Ellis, one of the surgeon's mates.[14]

At daylight on February 4th, having salted thirty-nine puncheons of fresh pork for a sea stock, and with sails and rigging newly mended, Cook directed the ships northward along the Kona coast. It was the winter season when the Kona wind

14. On Hawaiian birds see Scott B. Wilson and A. H. Evans, *Aves Hawaiienses: The Birds of the Sandwich Islands* (London, 1890-1899). William Ellis's drawing of the extinct Sandwich Rail is reproduced in color in this volume. George Forster published the first technical description of a native Hawaiian bird from four skins of the scarlet iiwi that were brought to Cassel, Germany, by B. Lohmann, one of the two sailors who had been lost for a day or two on Christmas Island.

sometimes gathers furious strength, and in one of these gales the foremast of the *Resolution* was sprung so badly that Cook reluctantly ordered the two ships back to Kealakekua Bay.

The tempo of thievery seemed to increase, though it had been a problem all along. Twice in one day the armourer's tongs were stolen from the *Discovery*, and at dawn on February 14th Lieutenant Burney, the officer of the watch, reported that the *Discovery's* large cutter had been stolen during the night. Captain Cook went ashore at once with Lieutenant Molesworth Phillips and nine marines under arms and attempted to seize King Kalaniopuu as a hostage. Soon Captain Clerke and Lieutenant Burney, waiting on board the *Discovery*, were alarmed at hearing a volley of small-arms fire and a violent shout from the natives. Looking through his telescope, Burney saw Captain Cook receive a blow and fall into the water.

Across the bay Lieutenant King was on shore at the astronomers' tents, where the ships' carpenters were still at work on the foremast of the *Resolution*, and so Captain Clerke sent William Bligh with a strong party to reinforce them and bring the mast on board.

> I never before felt such agitation [said Lieutenant King] as on seeing at last our cutter coming on shore, with Mr. Bligh. He called out before he reached the shore, to strike the observatories as quick as possible, and before he announced to us the shocking news that Captn Cook was killed, we saw it in his and the sailors' looks.[15]

15. The circumstances leading up to Cook's death are carefully reconstructed by J. C. Beaglehole, "The Death of Captain Cook," *Historical Studies: Australia and New Zealand*, Vol. 11, No. 43 (October 1964), pp. 289-305. See also Rupert T. Gould, "Some Unpublished Accounts of Cook's Death," *The Mariner's Mirror*, Vol. 14, No. 4 (October 1928), pp. 301-319.

Tempers on both sides gradually cooled during the ensuing week, though a party under Lieutenant Rickman's command set fire to a native village and bayonetted and decapitated several of the inhabitants. The bodies of the four marines who had been killed with Captain Cook were never recovered, and a peace emissary sent by King Kalaniopuu intimated that Cook's body had been accorded the treatment reserved for the bodies of high-ranking Hawaiian chiefs, the flesh being stripped from the bones. A bundle wrapped in a feathered cloak was eventually brought off to the ships and was found to contain some of Cook's remains—his hands, both arms, his skull, and the scalp with the ears attached. At sunset on Sunday, February 21, 1779, with the ships' flags at half mast and the guns firing at intervals, these remains of Captain Cook were committed to the deep. The next day, before the two ships sailed from Hawaii under Captain Clerke's command, a native chief returned Cook's lower jaw and his feet.

After collecting hogs and yams at Kauai and Niihau, the ships sailed northward for Kamchatka in order to carry out Cook's plan for a second Arctic exploration. Ropes and sails were continually giving way now, and the sheathing on the bows was beginning to come off. As April turned to May, the ships came to anchor in Avacha Bay at the harbor of Petropavlovsk, a desolate little fortress of log houses and conical huts on poles. Izmailov's letters were presented to the sergeant in command, and though the Russians were extremely suspicious of these foreign ships, Lieutenant King and John Webber, who could speak German, set out by dogsled to see the Governor of Kamchatka, who resided across the peninsula at

Bolcheretsk. During their absence, William Bligh made a survey of the harbor, and the crewmen seined for herring and gathered nettle tops and wild onions for their broth. The German-speaking Governor, Major Magnus von Behm, returned to Petropavlovsk with Webber and King and visited the English ships. He brought presents of tea and sugar for the officers and tobacco for the sailors, and at Captain Clerke's request he arranged for twenty head of cattle and quantities of flour to be sent from Bolcheretsk. Inasmuch as Major Behm was soon to return to St. Petersburg, Captain Clerke entrusted Cook's journal as well as his own to the Major's care, for delivery to the English ambassador. It was in this way that word of Cook's death first reached England in January of 1780.

Despite the rapid decline of his own health—he was dying from tuberculosis—Captain Clerke took the weary ships into the Arctic Ocean once again and followed the ice edge from one continent to the other. This year the ice, moving early, stretched farther south, and the ships were turned back some miles short of the point Cook had reached eleven months earlier. A Northeast or Northwest passage was clearly impractical for such ships.

At daybreak on August 21st the coast of Kamchatka was again in view, and that same morning Captain Clerke died. He was buried on the north side of the harbor at Petropavlovsk, near the grave of Louis Delisle de la Croyère, the French scientist who had sailed with Chirikov on Bering's second voyage. John Gore took command of the *Resolution* and James King moved up to command the *Discovery*. The naval stores promised by Major Behm eventually arrived from Okhotsk, and

67

having reclaimed a drummer boy who tried to desert with a Kamchadale girl, the ships sailed out of Avacha Bay just as winter was setting in.

Through gales and hazy weather the ships passed the Kurile Islands and sailed eastward of Japan, with just a glimpse of Mount Fujiyama. Iwo Jima was sighted in mid-November, and by early December they had reached the old Portuguese city of Macao, opposite Hong Kong. Captain King noticed the arched rock overlooking the sea where the poet Camoëns was said to have composed the *Lusiad*, and he made his way to Canton and brought back some English periodicals. The seamen, meanwhile, found they could sell their sea-otter skins to the Chinese merchants for fabulous prices. "The rage with which our seamen were possessed to return to Cook's River [said King], and, by another cargo of skins, to make their fortunes, at one time, was not short of mutiny." This commercial experience on Cook's third voyage led to the development of the maritime fur trade in which vessels, chiefly from Boston, collected sea-otter skins at Nootka Sound, refreshed at the Hawaiian Islands, where they sometimes took on cargoes of sandalwood, and then sailed to an avid market in Canton.[16]

Late in January, 1780, heading homeward, the ships stopped for a week at Con Son Island off South Vietnam and then sailed past Sumatra and through the Sunda Strait. Here John Webber made drawings of scenes on Krakatoa, a volcanic island which was to explode in 1883 in a cataclysmic eruption. After a month at Capetown, Captain Gore took the ships

16. See F. W. Howay, "An Outline Sketch of the Maritime Fur Trade," *Annual Report of the Canadian Historical Association* (1932), pp. 5-14.

around Ireland, waited for a favorable wind at Stromness in the Orkney Islands, and on October 4, 1780, the *Resolution* and *Discovery* concluded one of the longest exploring voyages in history.

In the interval of more than three and a half years that elapsed between the end of this voyage and the publication of the official account, four unauthorized narrative accounts made an appearance. The first of these was published anonymously but has since been attributed to Lieutenant John Rickman.[17] It was a catchpenny production and has some fanciful embellishments. A contemporary review, for example, noted that "the narrative is enlivened by a love-adventure between a youth of the *Discovery* and a Zealander girl." For an eager public, however, it did outline the contours of the voyage.

The second account was published in Germany in 1781 by Heinrich Zimmermann, who had been a lower-deck sailor on the *Discovery*.[18] It is a highly-compressed and somewhat ingenuous account, of which no English translation was published until 1926.[19]

17. [John Rickman], *Journal of Captain Cook's Last Voyage to the Pacific Ocean.* . . . (London, 1781). A facsimile reprint was published in Amsterdam in 1967. The attribution to Lieutenant Rickman is made by F. W. Howay, "Authorship of the Anonymous Account of Captain Cook's Last Voyage," *Washington Historical Quarterly*, Vol. 12, No. 1 (January 1921), pp. 51-58.

18. *Heinrich Zimmermanns von Wissloch in der Pfalz, Reise um die Welt, mit Capitain Cook* (Mannheim, 1781). A modern edition was published in Munich in 1966.

19. [Heinrich Zimmermann] *Zimmermann's Account of the Third Voyage of Captain Cook, 1776-1780*, transl. U. Tewsley (Wellington, N.Z., 1926; Alexander Turnbull Library, Bulletin No. 2). A second translation into English appeared four years later: *Zimmermann's Captain Cook*, transl. by Elsa Michaelis and Cecil French; ed. with introduction and notes by F. W. Howay (Toronto, 1930).

William Ellis, a surgeon's mate who had served on both the *Discovery* and the *Resolution,* published his two-volume account of the voyage in 1782.[20] David Samwell remarked of Ellis that "he tells no lies 'tis true but then he does not tell you half the odd adventures we met with; it is an unentertaining outline of the voyage." Ellis's volumes are illustrated with engravings of some twenty of his own drawings. He had artistic talent, and during the voyage he made more than one hundred natural-history drawings, chiefly of birds. For the most part these remain in the British Museum, unpublished.[21]

The fourth unauthorized account of the voyage was done by the American corporal of marines, John Ledyard. It was published in Hartford in 1783, with a dedication to Governor Jonathan Trumbull of Connecticut.[22] Opinion regarding it ranges from Henry R. Wagner's assertion that it is "a little masterpiece" to J. C. Beaglehole's condemnation of it as "a worthless production." It is probably safe to say that the book is more useful for the light it sheds on Ledyard than for the

20. William Ellis, *An Authentic Narrative of a Voyage . . . in Search of a North-West Passage . . .* (London, 1782). A facsimile reprint was published in Amsterdam in 1969.

21. [*115 Original Water-Colour Sketches of Animals Made by W. W. Ellis on Cook's Third Voyage, 1776-1780*]. Album in the Zoology Library of the British Museum (Natural History). The National Maritime Museum, Greenwich, owns ten of Ellis's watercolor paintings of landscapes of Pacific islands, and others are in the National Library of Australia, Canberra.

22. John Ledyard, *A Journal of Captain Cook's Last Voyage to the Pacific Ocean, and in Quest of a North-West Passage . . .* (Hartford, 1783). A facsimile reprint was published in Chicago in 1963 by Quadrangle Books, and a modern edition with introduction and notes is available: *John Ledyard's Journal of Captain Cook's Last Voyage,* ed. James K. Munford (Corvallis, Oregon, 1963).

information it provides about Cook's third voyage. On two counts Ledyard's journal has a place in the history of American publishing. It has claim to being the first book printed in America relating to the Northwest coast; and it has claim to being the first book copyrighted in the United States.[23] There is an element of irony in this latter claim, since fragments of Ledyard's book were plagiarized from Hawkesworth's *Voyages* and the concluding thirty-eight pages are lifted verbatim from Lieutenant Rickman's published account.

The long-awaited official account of the voyage was published in June, 1784, in three volumes accompanied by an atlas of more than sixty illustrations, and all copies were reportedly sold within three days.[24] Canon John Douglas, who had edited Cook's journal of the second voyage, was also editor of these. The first two volumes were based on Cook's manuscript, with interpolations from the journal of William Anderson, and the third volume was composed by Captain James King, who drew to some extent upon the journal of David Samwell.

The maps in the official account were based for the most part upon the surveys of Cook or of William Bligh. Despite his relative neglect by the official account, Bligh claimed that

23. See Hellmut Lehmann-Haupt, *The Book in America* (New York, 1939), pp. 88-92.

24. James Cook and James King, *A Voyage to the Pacific Ocean . . . for Making Discoveries in the Northern Hemisphere. . . .* 3 vols. (London, 1784). George Forster's preface to his German translation of these volumes (Berlin, 1787-88) is a significant essay. Portions of it have been made available in English by M. E. Hoare, " 'Cook the Discoverer': An Essay by Georg Forster, 1787," *Records of the Australian Academy of Science,* Vol. 1, No. 4 (November 1969), pp. 7-16.

"every plan and chart from the time of Cook's death, are exact copies of my work."[25] The sixty or more illustrations were engraved from the drawings of John Webber, who in subsequent years became known as a landscape painter and a regular exhibitor at the Royal Academy.[26]

Cook's journal from the third voyage has recently been re-edited from the original manuscript by J. C. Beaglehole.[27] Beaglehole also prints the surviving portions of William Anderson's journal separately in an appendix, and one of the gems of his edition is its inclusion of the complete journal of David Samwell. Samwell's essay on the death of Cook has long been known,[28] but, incredibly, his journal has here its first complete publication. In addition to proficiency in medicine, Samwell had a measure of literary talent. His copy of Horace went with him on Cook's voyage, and he could be moved to com-

25. Rupert T. Gould, "Bligh's Notes on Cook's Last Voyage," *The Mariner's Mirror*, Vol. 14 (1928), p. 371. Bligh is known to have kept a journal on Cook's third voyage, but it has never come to light. Possibly it was among the fifteen-year accumulation of Bligh's papers carried off by the mutineers on the *Bounty*. See Owen Rutter, *Turbulent Journey: A Life of William Bligh, Vice-Admiral of the Blue* (London, 1936), p. 35.

26. For a list of some fifty works exhibited by Webber between 1784 and 1792, see Algernon Graves, *The Royal Academy of Arts; a Complete Dictionary of Contributors and Works*, Vol. 8 (London, 1904), pp. 186-187. In addition to views in the South Seas, he painted landscapes in Wales, Switzerland, France, and Italy, including Pliny's villa on Lake Como. Sixteen additional plates of Pacific views, etched and colored by Webber, were issued separately between 1788 and 1792; these were re-engraved as colored aquatints and published as a set by Boydell in 1808 under the title *Views in the South Seas*.

27. J. C. Beaglehole, ed., *The Journals of Captain James Cook on His Voyages of Discovery, Vol. 3: The Voyage of the* Resolution *and* Discovery, *1776-1780* (Cambridge, 1967).

28. David Samwell, *A Narrative of the Death of Captain James Cook . . .* (London, 1786). A modern edition, with an introduction by Sir Maurice Holmes, has appeared under the title *Captain Cook and Hawaii* (San Francisco, 1957).

pose stanzas of verse after visiting the grave of the novelist Laurence Sterne.[29] It is fitting that Samwell's narrative of the third voyage should at last become available as a part of that cornerstone of modern Cook studies, the Beaglehole edition of Cook's journals.

29. On Samwell's career see William Davies, "David Samwell (1751-1798), Surgeon of the 'Discovery,' London-Welshman and Poet," *The Transactions of the Honourable Society of Cymmrodorion* (Session 1926-27), pp. 70-133.

INDEX

Index

77

Index

79

Of this book five thousand, five hundred copies
have been printed on
Mohawk superfine, soft-white eggshell paper.
The end-papers are linen Spectro, cocoaberry text,
and the cloth binding is Joanna Arrestox B linen.
The book is set in Linotype Janson
patterned after the 17th century original,
known for its readability, mellowness of form,
and evenness of color in mass.

Designed, printed, and bound at
The Lakeside Press
R. R. Donnelley & Sons Company
Chicago, Illinois and Crawfordsville, Indiana